THESE 3 WORDS...

WELCOME TO RACISM

DANA R STEVENS

I dedicate this book…

To my incredible parents, whose unwavering love and guidance have shaped every aspect of my being. This book is dedicated to you both, a tribute to the profound impact you have had on my life.

Dad, Edward, your presence in my life was a gift beyond measure. The qualities and characteristics you bestowed upon me fill me with immense pride. Your ability to make others feel valued, your generous heart, and the radiant light that emanated from you wherever you went—these are the qualities I strive to posses. When I last saw you, I made a promise to make you proud of the person I have become. It is my hope that this book will honor that desire. Since Covid-19 released your spirit, life has never been the same. I love you, Dad, and your memory lives on in my heart.

Mom, Lolita, you have been my steadfast companion, walking alongside me through every step of my journey. You have carried me through the challenges life has thrown our way, providing unwavering support and faith that has sustained me in times of darkness. Your love for me has been a constant source of strength, never faltering. Thank you for surrendering me to God, allowing Him to work in and through me. I am eternally grateful for the role you have played as my mother, and I cherish you deeply.

To both of you, Mom and Dad, I express my deepest gratitude for the pivotal roles you have played in shaping the person I am today. Your love, guidance, and unwavering belief in me have been the cornerstone of my journey. This book stands as a testament to the influence you have had on my life and the legacy you continue to leave behind. Thank you for everything.

With all my love,
Your Son, Dana (Big Poop, as Dad called me!)

CONTENTS

INTRODUCTION

I n a world plagued by the insidious grip of racism, few are willing to confront its true nature. But within the pages of my gripping memoir, I invite you to embark on an extraordinary journey through the tapestry of my life, woven against the backdrop of Chicago.

Prepare to be enthralled as my story unravels with unexpected twists and turns, each revelation challenging the very foundations of your beliefs. With unflinching honesty and raw vulnerability, I peel back the layers to expose the deep-rooted truths about racism that society often overlooks.

This is not a tale for the faint-hearted. It is a fearless exploration that dares you to step outside your comfort zone and confront the uncomfortable realities we all too often shy away from. Emotions will surge and intertwine as I fearlessly share the triumphs and struggles that have shaped me into the person I am today.

Through vivid descriptions and heartfelt narratives, I will transport you into the heart of my experiences. You will witness firsthand the realities of a small town upbringing, the tumultuous encounters with racial diversity, and the profound impact of a spiritual journey that forever altered my perception of the world.

This is a story of resilience, love, and the untapped power that lies within each of us when we choose to embrace the unknown. Brace yourself for a rollercoaster ride that will leave an indelible mark on your heart and mind.

So, my fellow truth-seekers, buckle up, keep your emotions close, and allow the power of my words to take you on an unforgettable ride through the depths of racial prejudice. Together, let us unearth the truth that lies beneath the surface and forge a path towards a brighter, more inclusive future.

FROM THE WILDERNESS

Let me take you on a heartfelt journey, beginning with the first 18 years of my life. As the eldest among my siblings, my family expanded quickly, with each new arrival adding a unique dynamic to our lives. Growing up in the idyllic town of St. James in southern Minnesota, our close-knit community of 4,500 people felt like an extended family. Yet, beneath the surface of our seemingly harmonious existence our little town had its hierarchy of important people to those on the bottom known as "white trailer trash". However, beneath this group of people were the only people of color living in our town, the Mexicans!

In my small town, with a graduating class of only 68 students and a total student population of around 500 from 7th to 12th grade, diversity was scarce. In my class there were just two Mexican students, Laura and Jessie. Laura, living at the end of my block, became a dear friend. Her parents, facing language barriers, worked tirelessly to provide for their family, their unwavering determination evident in their every step.

But the weight of racial prejudice hung heavily in the air, even in the innocence of childhood. The term "Mexican" became intertwined with negative connotations, forever tinged with the damning phrase, "Those damn Mexicans." To distance myself from this derogatory language, I resorted to using "Latinos" to refer to my friends, an attempt to alleviate the discomfort that lingered within me.

In the playground, during recess or gym class, we often relied on a counting-out rhyme to choose participants for games. Little did we know the roots of this seemingly innocent chant, which held a racial epithet within its words. Placing our right foot into the circle, we recited, "Eeny, meeny, miny, moe, Catch a Ni*** by the toe. If he hollers, make him pay. My momma told me you are not it!" It was a rhyme we mindlessly repeated, oblivious to its harmful implications, even in the presence of our teachers.

One memory etched in my mind dates back to my days in 5th or 6th grade, gathered with my family at my grandparents' home, watching a sporting event. Amidst the excitement, a shocking and hurtful remark slipped from the lips of one of my uncles. He used a racial slur "Goddamn no good Ni***" to describe Stevie Wonder, a talented and blind musician performing before our eyes. The contradiction struck me deeply, a confusion brewing within me. How could someone utter such hateful words toward a man who, despite his blindness, had achieved greatness far beyond what my uncle, with his sight intact, could ever imagine? The weight of that moment lingered, as I grappled with the jarring realization of racism ingrained in my own family.

Growing up in this insular town, devoid of cultural differences, I did not encounter a Black individual until I was 21 years old, long after leaving my hometown. It was a shocking revelation, shining a spotlight on the racial ignorance that permeated my formative years. But within this recognition lies the crux of my story—a journey of self-discovery, personal growth, and an unwavering pursuit of truth. Racism was so deeply embedded in our lives, like swimming in saltwater, its presence so normalized that we failed to recognize the corrosive effects it had on our hearts and minds.

Amidst the backdrop of my upbringing, my family played an integral role in shaping who I am today. Gatherings at Grandma's house during holidays remain etched in my memory, filled with laughter and cherished moments. However, as time passed and our grandparents departed, the ties that bound us together began to loosen. These days, our reunions are infrequent, reserved for bittersweet occasions such as weddings and funerals.

Step into the intimate tapestry of my childhood, where the unconditional love of my parents painted vibrant strokes across our lives. Within the walls of our home, my mom's heart overflowed with boundless affection, earning her the endearing title of "Grandma" to the children she served as a head cook. From the homemade lunches she lovingly prepared to the warmth in her words and embraces, she emanated a nurturing presence that left an indelible imprint on the hearts of those around her. I still witness the tears welling up in her eyes as she recounts the stories of those precious children who faced unimaginable hardships. Her compassionate heart, overflowing with a genuine desire to make a difference, has become the compass that guides my own journey.

My mom, a culinary wizard, wove magic in the kitchen, conjuring mouthwatering dishes and delightful sweets that tantalized our taste buds. The aroma of Sunday dinners permeated our home, etching memories in our minds as we attended church. Roast, potatoes, carrots, and her frozen homemade cream corn were the secret ingredients that nourished our bodies and nurtured our souls, helping us grow big and strong. Among her culinary creations, her Chocolate Chip Cookies and homemade Chocolate Cake will always hold a special place in my heart, a treasured delight that still brings warmth to my soul.

But my mom's love extended far beyond her culinary talents. Our house was a sanctuary of cleanliness and order, meticulously maintained by her hands. She enlisted my help in rearranging the living room, hanging new pictures, or giving the existing ones a fresh arrangement, instilling in me a love for creating a warm and inviting space. I inherited her keen eye for aesthetics, an enduring legacy that blossoms in the spaces I now inhabit.

My mom's multifaceted gifts extended beyond the boundaries of our home, yet her self-esteem often hindered their full expression. During my middle school years, she showcased her creativity by selling various crafts at local bazaars and craft shows. As she focused on her craft business, I found solace in the basement, diligently crafting wooden objects with precision for her to paint. Though remnants of those creative endeavors remain tucked away in our attic, what lingers most profoundly is the shared bond of creativity we fostered, a testament to the love that wove us together.

My father, a pillar of dedication, spent 32 years working tirelessly for UPS, enduring scorching summers and freezing winters to provide for our family. He exemplified unwavering commitment, leaving for work early each morning and returning late at night. Yet, amidst the demands of his labor, he chose to invest his precious time with us, valuing family over fleeting pleasures. His love and devotion knew no bounds, leaving an indelible impression on my heart.

Meticulous and skilled, my father took immense pride in our home, our yard, and his cars. His meticulous car care routine became legendary in our little town, earning him the reputation of the fussiest and pickiest car owner around. Yet, beyond his meticulous nature, he exuded a contentment that defied envy and jealousy. Material possessions held little sway over his heart, and he embraced gratitude for what he had while appreciating the blessings bestowed upon others.

My parents ensured that we attended church every weekend, except during summers when we embarked on camping adventures. Albion Lutheran Church became our spiritual home for most of my formative years. In my 7th and 8th grade, I participated in confirmation classes, attending every Wednesday night. Upon completion, family and friends gathered to witness our public affirmation of baptism during a Sunday service. As part of this milestone, we each chose a Bible verse to memorize and share with the congregation. Little did I know that God was already preparing me for the remarkable journey that lay ahead. The verse I selected was from 1 John 4:7-8: "Beloved, let us love one another, for love comes from God. Everyone who loves has been born of God and knows God. Whoever does not love does not know God because God is love."

Together, my parents crafted a childhood adorned with unforgettable camping adventures. From a humble tent to a cozy pop-up camper and finally an RV with a bathroom, we journeyed through Cedar Grove, the Black Hills, and Madeline Island. The memories we forged in that close-knit space remain etched in my mind, a testament to the blessings that graced my upbringing.

In the embrace of my parents' love, my siblings and I never doubted the depths of their devotion. Sacrifices were made without hesitation, as they prioritized our needs above their own. Even if it meant putting back a new shirt or a pair of pants, their selflessness knew no bounds. Their love manifested not only in spoken words but in countless acts of warmth and care, touching the lives of all fortunate enough to be in their presence.

As I reflect upon the incredible souls who shaped my world, I am filled with gratitude. My beloved father, Edward Dale Stevens, now rests in eternal peace, his presence forever cherished as Covid-19 claimed him in November 2021. Yet, the legacy of love he and my mom, Lolita Kay Stevens (Even), bestowed upon me endures. Their selflessness, their unwavering devotion, and their genuine care for others serve as guiding stars, inspiring me to navigate life's challenges with compassion and grace. Within their remarkable hearts, I discovered the strength and resilience that have propelled me forward on this extraordinary journey called life.

I will forever hold dear the cherished memories with my devoted Christian grandparents, especially those days spent with my Grandma Stevens. Her unwavering faith and dedication shone brightly as she faithfully served as a Sunday School teacher for over two decades. It was under her gentle guidance that a deep yearning to know God was planted within my young heart.

Witnessing Grandma's love and compassion unfold in her classroom left an indelible mark on my soul. I recall a poignant moment when I questioned her decision to offer candy to a little boy who had been misbehaving. Her response, spoken with unwavering kindness, reverberated within me: "Oh Dana, it's those who need love the most." Those words, imbued with profound wisdom, have become the compass that steers my life's journey, urging me to embody them in every interaction and choice I make.

Grandma Stevens' unconditional love taught me that amidst the complexities of life, extending compassion to those who may struggle or act out is a transformative act. It is a philosophy that has become the cornerstone of my existence, guiding me to embrace empathy, understanding, and grace in my interactions with others.

As I reflect upon those treasured memories of Grandma and Grandpa Even and Grandma and Grandpa Stevens, and the invaluable lessons imparted by my them, my heart swells with gratitude for the enduring legacy they bestowed upon me. Their influence continues to shape my path, inspiring me to navigate life's twists and turns with unwavering love and unwavering faith. It is through their live examples and the sacred connection I shared with them that I strive to make a positive impact in the lives of others, one compassionate act at a time.

In the scorching July of 1990, the summer before my senior year in high school, my childhood friends from two houses down invited me to the Sonshine Festival. This incredible event, held outdoors near Willmar, Minnesota, can only be described as a "Christian Woodstock." Over 15,000 people flocked to this gathering, eagerly anticipating performances by renowned contemporary Christian artists like The Newsboys, DC Talk, and Petra. The festival culminated with Michael W. Smith's performance on Saturday night. It was during his final song, "Pray for Me," that God reached out and seized my heart. As the words "One day love will bring us back around" reverberated through the air, I found myself transported from the crowd, longing to experience that love for myself. In that very moment, I felt something extraordinary enter my being, leaving me awestruck. When I finally regained my senses, I discovered myself on my knees, about 20 feet in front of the stage. I have no recollection of how I navigated through the sea of nearly 10,000 people to reach that crowded spot. From that moment on, my life was forever transformed.

From my seventh grade year to this point of time, I grappled privately with deep depression and thoughts of suicide. I had even devised three different ways to end my life and came dangerously close to acting upon one of them. But then, God reached out to me, declaring His love. Upon returning home from the Sonshine Festival, I purged my life of secular music, bidding farewell to bands like Def Leppard and Quiet Riot. My heart had undergone a profound change, and now, all I desired was to live a life used by God to bring hope to the hopeless, just as I had been when He touched my soul.

Later that summer, in 1990, I had the opportunity to MC the St. James Jr. Miss Pageant. It was there that I met one of the contestants who would become my girlfriend during my senior year in high school. Her father, a Lutheran pastor, held family Bible studies nearly six days a week, and I gladly attended each one. God had orchestrated this encounter, providing me with a loving and supportive foundation to further strengthen my relationship with Him. I will forever cherish the Westendorf family for embracing me and guiding me on my spiritual journey during my senior year in high school.

During my senior year, as a young and proud American, I fervently supported our troops fighting in the Gulf War. Our home, nestled across from Memorial Park, held a front-row seat to the ebb and flow of the park with St James lake as the backdrop. In the eyes of us teenagers, our street was a part of "The Whip," a designated route where we would cruise in our cars, seeking a taste of coolness in the midst of St. James' limited offerings.

Along the Dike Road, separating the serene lake from Memorial Park, served as a gathering point for us teens to hang out. But for me, the allure of this spot held a potential danger. Drinking was often part of the scene, and the watchful eyes of my father meant that lingering there could have dire consequences.

Amidst the backdrop of my senior year, as the war raged on, a seed of inspiration took root within me. I decided to transform our neighborhood block into "A Block of Support" for our brave troops. With unwavering determination, I crafted signs bearing the names of each soldier from St. James and neighboring towns, proudly displaying them in the yards of each home along the street. My intention was clear—to ensure that anyone passing by, whether strolling through the park or driving down our block, would be reminded of the sacrifices made by our soldiers and encouraged to support them, especially those hailing from our local community.

As each soldier returned safely home, a small American flag adorned their name sign, a symbol of their triumph and our collective relief. The impact of this gesture rippled through our town, catching the attention of various news outlets and newspapers. They sought to capture the essence of my patriotism, sharing stories that touched the hearts of readers far and wide.

The echoes of my support reached beyond the boundaries of our streets. I was invited to lend my voice to the welcome home celebrations organized by our city, standing before the crowds to sing in honor of our returning heroes. These experiences further ignited my passion and dedication, instilling in me a deep appreciation for the sacrifices made by our soldiers and the power of unity in supporting them.

In a poignant culmination to my senior year, both the VFW and Legion recognized my unwavering commitment. They awarded me scholarships for college, acknowledging the impact of my endeavors and affirming the significance of unity and support in times of adversity.

Looking back, those moments of rallying the community, honoring our troops, and spreading a message of unity remain etched in my heart. They serve as a testament to the power of a collective spirit, reminding us that even in a small town like St. James, we can make a difference and uplift those who fight for our freedom.

Before I knew it, my senior year flew by, and I found myself venturing off to college. I decided to attend Waldorf College, a small two-year institution nestled in the charming town of Forest City, Iowa. Though similar in size to St. James, this college town boasted a few additional perks. I was fortunate to receive a small scholarship for my involvement in drama and choir. During my sophomore year, I even had the honor of being elected as the president of Waldorf College Choir.

Initially, I had set my sights on pursuing a pre-med major. The deep love I held for animals had propelled me toward the dream of becoming a veterinarian, dedicating my life to their well-being. However, my aspirations in that field came crashing down even before my first year of college drew to a close. Firstly, the vast amount of information proved overwhelming for my brain to handle. Secondly, God had stripped away my tolerance for blood. Even today, the sight of a single drop can still send me reeling.

But my love for helping those in pain extended beyond animals to people, particularly young individuals. As the oldest child, I often yearned for an older brother figure who could impart words of wisdom as I navigated through the uncharted territories of life. Through my experiences, I became the trailblazer for my younger siblings, making the mistakes so that they could learn from them and forge their own paths.

The summer of 1992 brought me to the breathtaking wilderness of Northern Minnesota, where I embarked on a thrilling adventure as a camp counselor at a Bible Camp. Eager to immerse myself in the experience, I even learned how to play the guitar to lead worship sessions around the crackling campfire. But that was just the beginning. I led campers on daring canoe trips deep into the untamed wilderness, far from the comforts of electricity, plumbing, and showed the youth how to protect themselves from the wild beasts lurking nearby. To safeguard our food from these curious creatures, we ingeniously hung it in the trees, ensuring a peaceful night's sleep, albeit with a touch of fear lingering in the air. It took several nights for most campers to overcome their trepidation, but the unforgettable memories we created amidst the wilderness solidified my passion for working with youth, inspiring me to aspire to become a Bible Camp Director in such a remarkable setting.

As my college journey progressed into my Sophomore year, I assumed the role of Resident Assistant, responsible for overseeing the second floor of Rasmusson Hall. Late August brought the return of the Resident Assistants for training and preparations before the students arrived for the fall semester. During one of our final gatherings, we ventured to a farm for a delightful grill-out and an exhilarating game of volleyball. Little did I know that this seemingly innocent game would take an unexpected turn. As I leaped into the air, poised to make an impressive volley, fate had other plans. My legs went up, causing me to land awkwardly on my wrist, resulting in a compound break. The nearest hospital was over an hour away, and due to the severity of the break, I was transferred to another hospital, adding more hours to the agonizing wait. Finally, after nearly five hours, I received my first cast of several, extending all the way til graduation! Thus, my sophomore year commenced with an unexpected twist, but I faced it with resilience and determination.

Ah, the exhilaration and recklessness of youth! One Friday night in March, filled with daring spirit, Tony, two ladies, and I, with my cast, decided to indulge in some nighttime sledding. Ignoring the darkness that enveloped us, we set off for a hill outside of Forest City, ready to conquer its icy slopes. Tony, ever the daredevil, volunteered to sled down first to "make a path" and ensure our safety. To our collective bewilderment, Tony chose an unconventional method, sliding down on his stomach, headfirst. Little did we know that this innocent thrill-seeking would turn into a chilling nightmare. The moment his face scraped against the icy surface, screams of pain filled the air. Blood stained the snow, leaving behind a terrifying trail. Our immediate instinct was to rush him to the emergency room, fearing the worst. The mere thought of blood would usually incapacitate me, but during this blood-soaked ordeal, it was only by God's grace that

I remained steadfast. Images of a blood-covered Tony still haunt my memories, and my stomach churns at the recollection. Fortunately, his nose and lips remained intact, though his face bore the scars of the harrowing incident. Needless to say, we never attempted such reckless adventures again.

Waldorf College, unfortunately, reflected the same lack of diversity I experienced in my hometown. The campus was predominantly white, with only a few African students studying abroad, seeking education to bring back to their home countries. As I sat in the cafeteria, my gaze would often be drawn to the small group of black students, primarily male athletes on sports scholarships, gathered together at a table tucked away in the corner. A palpable divide seemed to exist, leaving little room for meaningful interaction between our black and white peers. It was a somber reminder of the profound impact that racism had forged, creating barriers and isolating individuals based on the color of their skin.

And just like that, my time at Waldorf College drew to a close. A dear friend named Jody, who had graduated the previous year, returned to witness my graduation ceremony. As we strolled through the campus one last time, we unexpectedly crossed paths with Professor Orr. Though I didn't personally know him, Jody had served as his assistant during her time at Waldorf. "Hi Jody! How good to see you! Did you know I'm leaving Waldorf to teach at Moody Bible Institute in Chicago?" These words struck a chord within me, for until that moment, I had no clear plans for the upcoming fall. I hadn't chosen a college to complete my final two years of education. But little did I know, God had already prepared a path for me.

"Professor Orr, what is Moody Bible Institute?" I inquired, my curiosity piqued. In the span of a thirty-minute conversation, Professor Orr unveiled the wonders of Moody and all it had to offer. What astounded me the most was the fact that Moody didn't charge tuition. This revelation flooded me with excitement and gratitude, for it seemed that divine intervention had paved the way for my next step. God hadn't let me down; He had merely stretched my faith, revealing my next move at the very last moment. A gospel song I have since added to my repertoire captures the essence of this experience: "He's an on-time God, yes He is! Job said, He may not come when you want Him, but He'll be there right on time. He's an on-time God, yes He is!"

That Spring just before I graduated, I remember a particular April day when I and a few classmates journeyed to the University of Iowa in Cedar Falls to apply for a coveted camp counselor position with the Camp Adventure program. This remarkable initiative provided college students with the opportunity to travel abroad and work with the various military branches offering summer camps for youth residing on those U.S. military bases across the globe. After a weekend of rigorous activities and interviews, I received the incredible news that I had been selected for a position in Ansbach, Germany. The prospect of embarking on this international adventure filled me with excitement and anticipation. Little did I know that this opportunity would shape my future in unimaginable ways.

In late May, the moment arrived for me to bid farewell to my parents as they accompanied me to Cedar Falls, Iowa. There, in the embrace of a relative, I found myself in the company of someone who would transport me to join my colleagues on that fateful Monday. Little did I know that the words she would utter during that car ride would leave an indelible mark on my soul.

As we drove past homes that bore the signs of hardship, their worn exteriors hinting at the struggles within, I noticed several black individuals seated on their porches. It was then that my relative turned to me with a cruel intention, piercing the air with her words. "You know what you're looking at, Dana, don't you?" Confusion clouded my mind as I responded, "No, what?" What followed was a statement that shattered my excitement and left me reeling in disbelief.

"A bunch of porch monkeys waiting for their welfare checks from you and me, and all of us white folks paying taxes for them lazy ass people!" Her words hung heavy in the air, staining my heart with their venomous racism. She dropped me off at my destination, where I joined ten other white staff members, embarking on a journey that would forever shape our lives. Our destination? Ansbach barracks in Ansbach, Germany, a place that would become our home for the summer. Some of us were assigned to Katterbach, while others ventured to Illesheim Army Base, both a mere 15-minute drive from the barracks.

That summer on each Friday once the last child was picked up, a sense of adventure gripped me. Whether I ventured alone or with a few companions, we hopped on trains, ready to explore cities and countries beyond the camp's boundaries. Among the myriad trips I embarked on, one that still stands out in my mind is my voyage to Rome. Accompanied by two female staff members—one blond, the other brunette—we embarked on a thrilling adventure. Little did we know that our journey would take an unexpected turn, filled with both fear and divine protection.

The train ride to Rome lasted well over 16 hours, but the captivating scenery made every minute worthwhile. As the train meandered through the majestic Swiss Alps, a breath-taking spectacle unfolded before our eyes. For nearly 45 minutes, we found ourselves completely immersed in the mountains, a sight that left us breathless. Eventually, we retired for the night in a sleep car, equipped with seats that could be transformed into makeshift beds. However, our slumber was abruptly interrupted when I awoke to hands attempting to access my zipped passport bag. Startled, we screamed, but before we could grasp the situation, the intruder vanished. Within minutes, the Train Conductor provided us with instructions on how to sleep safely. From then on, to ensure our security I slept in the middle of the cabin, with my legs propped up against the doors. If anyone attempted to open them, my legs would involuntarily fall, startling them and alerting me to their presence. Remarkably, all three of us resorted to sleeping with our legs guarding the doors, no one was gonna rob us!

Once we finally arrived in Rome, we found ourselves without a place to stay, a recurring theme in my travels. It's important to remember that in 1993, the internet and cell phones were not yet invented. But as always, God provided a way, gently guiding me on a path He had already laid out. Enter Amid, a kind-hearted Egyptian man who sensed our youth and bewilderment. and our lostness! To cut a long story short, he became our guardian angel. Amid accompanied us everywhere we desired to go, even to places he advised us to avoid. We made our way to the famous coliseum. We stood in front of the Vatican awaiting the pope's Sunday message. On one occasion, while we were returning from Ostia, the nearest beach to Rome, we stumbled upon a flea market. Against Amid's advice, we decided to explore it while he waited at a nearby coffee shop. Little did we know that danger lurked within those bustling market stalls.

As we perused shoes and clothing, the owner fixated his attention on Lisa, my blond friend. Within twenty minutes, it became clear that his interest in her had turned obsessive, and he didn't handle rejection well. Convinced that we were a couple and that I was hindering their relationship, he grew increasingly agitated. In a fit of anger, he yelled something in Italian, summoning three imposing men to forcefully open the back doors of their van. In that moment, divine intervention was our only refuge. God granted all three of us an unprecedented burst of speed as we fled toward our meeting place with Amid. Though we can't be certain of what transpired between Amid and the men, we hopped on a train, hiding in fear as it carried us back to Rome. The following day, we remained in Rome, nursing our shaken nerves before returning to Germany. We never saw Amid again, but I firmly believe he was our guardian angel.

I will forever cherish a conversation I had with a young lady around my age, twenty at the time. Despite her limited English skills, we managed to communicate effectively. During our exchange, I shared that it was my first time traveling to Switzerland, embarking on a solo journey to meet a friend in Basel. To my surprise, she revealed that this was also her first trip to Switzerland and only her third time venturing beyond the walls of East Germany.

Curiosity overwhelmed me, and I couldn't resist asking about her experiences living under communism. Did she find it frightening? Did she fear for her life? Her response left a lasting impression on me. "My greatest fear," she confessed, "was venturing beyond the confines of what I knew, the walls that had shielded me from the outside world for so long."

In that moment, I realized the significance of our conversation and how it tied into God's intricate plan for my life. Through her words, I would one day understand the power of indoctrination and the profound impact it has on me and you! How the wall of racism stands tall and strong here in America and how it blocks truth! This encounter served as a crucial lesson, a stepping stone on my journey of comprehension of the power of being indoctrinated, even when you don't think you are!

Before the summer drew to a close, I embarked on remarkable journeys to Paris, Amsterdam, Copenhagen, Prague, various cities in Switzerland and Austria, and throughout Germany. The summer camp had become a catalyst for my love of travel and exploration. However, there was one final trip I couldn't leave Europe without undertaking—an adventure to southern France to visit Axelle. She had been a foreign exchange student and a dear friend of my sister and our family during my junior year of high school. Thus, I embarked on a two-and-a-half-day train ride, which presented its own unexpected twist.

During the second night of my journey to Avignon, as I slept soundly in my seat, a stranger I had never laid eyes upon woke me abruptly. He informed me that I needed to move from the car at the end of the train to one of the first three cars. The car I was on would remain at the station, headed in the opposite direction. Without hesitation, I sprang into action, and to my surprise, he grabbed one of my suitcases, offering his assistance as we swiftly navigated through the train cars. With only a few minutes to spare, I made the transfer successfully. To this day, I marvel at the mysterious stranger's knowledge of my destination. It was as though he, too, was an angel, guiding me along my journey and preparing me for the future that awaited me. In the end, I spent two extraordinary weeks in southern France with Axelle and her family.

Throughout that summer, my conversations with my parents were infrequent, occurring just once every other week. During one of those phone calls in July, my mother read my acceptance letter for the Youth Ministry Degree at Moody Bible Institute. It was a moment of sheer joy and surprise, for I had been informed during the application process that there was typically a two-year waitlist for admission. Yet, against all odds, I received the green light to commence my studies that fall. However, since I wouldn't return home until mid-September, I decided to start in January of 1994 for the spring semester. In the interim, I moved back home and worked full-time, diligently saving money for the exciting chapter that lay ahead.

On January 2nd, 1994, my parents and I embarked on a journey from our small town of St. James to the bustling city of Chicago. To us small-town folks, Chicago carried a reputation of being unsafe and unfriendly. Yet, despite their concerns, my parents were remarkably supportive of my decision to attend Moody Bible Institute, even though it meant immersing myself in the city's urban environment. It was time for me to take the next step in following God's path for my life. Excitement coursed through me, though it was tempered by a touch of fear for a city where the entire population of my hometown could fit within one of its skyscrapers.

Moody's campus resided in the heart of downtown Chicago, nestled on the corner of Chicago Avenue and LaSalle Street. Just a short 10-15 minute walk away was the famed Magnificent Mile, and from there, an additional five minutes would bring me to the picturesque shores of Lake Michigan. The sight of the towering buildings and majestic skyscrapers that stretched for miles left an indelible mark on my memory. The sheer beauty of this man-made landscape made me wonder what astounding wonders man was capable of creating.

As I arrived on campus a few days before the official start of orientation, the atmosphere felt eerily quiet, with most students still on Christmas break. Thanks to the arrangements made by Professor Orr, I was able to settle into my dorm room early. My room happened to be located on the top floor, the 19th floor of Culbertson Hall, one of the men's dormitories. Standing with my parents, we gazed out the window at the breathtaking view of Chicago from this lofty vantage point. In the center of it all stood the majestic Sears Tower, towering 108 floors high. It was a sight that left us in awe. After a moment of silence, my mom broke the stillness, her voice quivering with emotion as she asked, "Will you like it here?"

Soon, the inevitable moment of goodbyes arrived, a heart-wrenching experience, especially for my mom. In a futile attempt to hold back tears, she would twitch her nose and mouth to the right, a gesture that had never succeeded in stopping the flood of emotions. I, on the other hand, remained composed and dry-eyed as I watched my parents drive away, their car blending into the sea of traffic. Turning around, I found myself in a surreal state, as if caught in a dream. Returning to my room, the solitude engulfed me, and tears began to flow. Once again, I gazed out the window, this time with only my thoughts as company. "No turning back now, Dana," I whispered to myself, knowing that my journey had truly begun.

THE IMPACT OF 3 WORDS

Moody Bible Institute, as I mentioned earlier, was nestled in the heart of downtown Chicago, within walking distance of iconic landmarks such as Lake Michigan, the Magnificent Mile, and the HardRock Cafe. During our orientation, they emphasized the importance of staying safe in this sprawling metropolis, particularly for those of us hailing from small rural towns. We were also informed about Cabrini Green, a notorious inner-city housing project located just a couple of blocks west of campus. The stark contrast between the affluent residents on one side and the impoverished inhabitants on the other side amazed me. It was a striking realization of how two completely different worlds coexisted mere blocks apart. This concept of "the other side of the tracks" that I had heard of growing up suddenly became tangible and undeniable. It was that side we were taught to stay away from.

By the second week of January, all the students had returned to campus after the Christmas break. As students pursuing careers in Christian ministry, one of our expectations was to find a church that would become our "home away from home" for worship. However, it was already March, and I had yet to find my place of worship. Part of the reason was my goal of securing a youth pastor position to gain hands-on experience while pursuing my degree. And of course, the extra income would be greatly appreciated.

During one of our floor meetings which always ended in prayer, I expressed my ongoing search for a church and a job. Two of my white floor mates (I mention their race for a specific reason) extended an invitation for me to join them at Rock of Our Salvation Church in the Austin Community on the west side of Chicago. I heard a few guys mutter "Oooo, the west side!" Being new to the city, I was oblivious to the reputation of different neighborhoods and had no preconceived notions. James and Ken, my friends, were Urban Ministry Majors. I was excited about this opportunity to visit a new church and hopefully find my "home away from home."

As I mentioned earlier, I had no prior knowledge of the city or experience riding the subway, let alone venturing to the west side. On that Sunday morning in March 1994, the second Sunday of the month, the three of us walked a few blocks from campus to the Chicago Subway stop. We boarded the Red Line, walked down some hallways and stair to transfer at Washington, and switched to the Blue Line headed towards Forest Park. I was grateful that my friends knew the way; otherwise, I might have been endlessly wandering through the labyrinth of subway tunnels in search of the correct train.

Austin was our stop, leaving only three more stops before reaching the end of the Blue Line. It was then that I began to understand the significance of those murmurs I had heard earlier. With each subsequent stop, more and more Caucasian passengers exited the train, until the three of us were the only ones left in that particular car when we reached our destination. Fear crept up within me momentarily, until I reminded myself that I was with my friends, who had been attending this church for years. I was in their company, so what was there to worry about, even if we were the only whites on this car?

I understand that you may be taken aback by my racially biased or stereotypical thoughts. However, it is crucial to consider my upbringing and the influences that shaped my perspective. The news and media often portrayed Black families and inner-city neighborhoods in a negative light, including what we referred to as "the ghetto." Additionally, I had a vivid memory from my childhood while my mom was driving and got lost in the inner-city of Kansas City. The fear that engulfed us during that experience left an indelible mark. We were instructed to lock the car doors, avoid eye contact, and quickly navigate through stop signs to prevent potential robberies. There was an underlying fear of being taken away if we were pulled over by authorities. This fear left a profound impact on me, and from that point on, my father assumed the role of the sole driver for our family's trips.

Now, with these memories and fears swirling in my mind, I was about to disembark from the train and embark on a several-block walk to the church. A part of me wanted to succumb to the anxiety and turn back, retreating to the safety of campus. But I was also too proud to let my friends see how afraid I truly was. So, I reassured myself that everything would be alright. After all, nothing had happened to them over all these years, and it was just a Sunday afternoon. Each step I took on that walk, my apprehension gradually eased, until we finally arrived at the church.

Rock of Our Salvation Church, established in 1983 by Pastor Raleigh Washington, prided itself on being a "multi-ethnic, multi-cultural, and economically diverse congregation" that celebrated the unique gifts and differences of its members. The church was dedicated to community outreach, racial reconciliation, missions, discipleship, and collaboration with like-minded organizations. Its primary focus was serving the needs of the Austin community, which was often marginalized and overlooked by society. Pastor

Washington's vision extended beyond the church itself, as he founded Circle Urban Ministry, a social service organization that provided essential support such as healthcare, legal services, counseling, and after-school programs.

Rock Church, with its hands-on approach to ministry, drew my friends from Moody Bible Institute. Pastor Washington's commitment to embodying the heart of Christ and fostering unity was exemplified in his book, co-authored with Glen Kehrein, titled "Breaking down Walls: A Model for Reconciliation in an Age of Racial Strife."

As I gazed upon the congregation, I noticed several individuals who shared my skin tone, making me feel less like an outsider in a sea of mostly black individuals. The church held its services in what doubled as a gym during the week but transformed into a sanctuary on Sundays. Everything had a dual purpose, but the underlying mission was to meet both the spiritual and physical needs of the community. This concept of a church centered around community rather than the worship service itself was entirely new to me, coming from a small country church called Albion Lutheran. Service at Albion lasted precisely one hour, with a brief hymn and minimal fanfare. Here, at Rock Church, the praise and worship alone lasted nearly 45 minutes! My eyes and mouth widened as I witnessed a form of worship I had never experienced before. It was over an hour before Pastor Washington stepped up to preach, and his sermons often extended beyond that hour. Back home, any pastor who dared to go even five to ten minutes over the hour mark would risk losing their congregation. In our small farming community, people had responsibilities, chores, and animals to tend to, and time was of the essence.

During my teenage years, while working at Hardee's, we offered free coffee to senior citizens during breakfast hours. I vividly remember the ire that erupted among these churchgoers when their pastor's sermon ran a few minutes over, causing them to miss out on their complimentary coffee. It baffled me how those who had just come from church could display such unkindness. It was experiences like these that led me to swear off attending church once I left home, but God!

Of course, my friends had neglected to mention this one small detail—the services at Rock Church were often hours long. But since this was my first encounter with a predominantly Black church, I found myself captivated by the music, the freedom of worship, the vibrant dancing, and the impassioned preaching. Above all, what truly touched my heart was the genuine love that permeated the atmosphere.

The message Pastor Washington delivered during the service was centered around how stereotypes kill people." He challenged us to confront the stereotypes we held about others, recognizing that these preconceived notions could be just as destructive as physical harm or hurtful words as it all begins in our minds and hearts. It didn't take a weapon or harsh language to destroy a person's life—our thoughts about them could be equally damaging. Pastor Washington implored us to dismantle negative stereotypes and view one another through the lens of Christ's love, rather than through the filters of media, societal expectations and our own families. This message deeply resonated with me, especially considering my upbringing in a racially homogeneous town. In my community, Mexicans were often derogatorily labeled, and it took years for me to shed the ingrained biases that prevented me from even saying the word Mexican without making me feel I was insulting them. Pastor Washington's words spoke to the core of my being as I planted the seeds of this teaching within my heart.

After the service, as we made our way back to the train station, a few inches of snow had fallen, making our journey somewhat treacherous. Walking single file, I trailed behind my friends, and about a block away up ahead, I noticed five young Black men heading towards us on the same path. Immediately, negative stereotypes flooded my mind. Thoughts of robbery and violence consumed me, and I contemplated running or at least crossing the street to ensure my safety. This was precisely why I had insisted on having a cell phone—so I could call for help in moments like these. But then, my heart reminded me of Pastor Washington's message. It posed a series of introspective questions: If those five young men were white, would I be thinking these things? Would I feel the same way? Did I have any personal experiences with Black people, positive or negative? Where did I derive these thoughts and feelings from? Were they rooted in stereotypes or truth? Thus, a fierce debate ensued within my mind and heart.

Then, God brought to mind the parable of the Farmer Scattering Seed from Matthew 13. He asked me, "Where is your heart, son? The choice is yours." In that moment, I made the decision to cultivate good soil within my heart, allowing those seeds of truth to take root and flourish. I was determined to conquer the negative stereotypes I had been taught and align my life with the example set by Christ.

Winter in Minnesota seemed to stretch from late October all the way to early June, and it was a season I barely tolerated. However, amidst the freezing temperatures and snowy landscapes, one skill I had mastered was building snowmen and engaging in epic snowball fights. Little did I know that the encounter I was about to have with these young men would be far from a friendly snowball fight. As I watched them gather ice chunks, a wave of concern washed over me, anticipating the imminent harm they would inflict upon those entering their snowball fight!

Approaching my two friends, these young men greeted them with a casual "What's up?" It was then that I understood how to respond appropriately. Summoning the voice of a white boy from rural Minnesota, I replied, "What is up?" But in the split second that those words left my lips, I was met with a brutal punch to my face. Before I could process what had just happened, I felt an ice chunk collide with the back of my head. A punch to my gut sent me crashing to the ground, where I was met with a kick and the venomous words, "Welcome to racism."

Both of my friends continued walking and conversing, oblivious to the violence unfolding behind them. It was only when those haunting words echoed through the air—"Welcome to racism"—that they stopped in their tracks, turning to find me in the snow, my nose streaming with blood and my spirit shattered. You may wonder, "Come on, Dana, how could your friends not have known you were being attacked?" But the truth is, they had no idea. This was my personal "Saul to Damascus experience," an encounter divinely orchestrated between God and me. It marked the beginning of a profound journey, one where I would strive to understand, to the best of my ability. It wasn't the physical pain I had just experienced from the hits, but the excruciating pain that inflicted my soul, the hidden pain beneath the cutting words of "Welcome to racism" that lied in the souls of those five young men!

THE JOURNEY BEGINS!

To claim that I never grappled with feelings of anger would be a falsehood. Just like the apostle Paul, I'm certain he faced his own inner battles, particularly during his time of blindness and the immense suffering he endured throughout his life in fulfilling his calling. Yet, the greatest pain I experienced, surpassing both physical and emotional torment, was the inner pain I felt by those five young men. I sensed a profound anguish emanating from that altercation, rooted in the insidious disease of racism. It gripped me tightly, refusing to let go, and at times, even intensified. The pain pierced my soul, driving me to embark on a quest to comprehend the nature and depth of racism.

At Moody Bible Institute, I immersed myself in various urban-focused groups. I joined the Unity of Praise Gospel Choir, where I eventually became the president in my second year. Although I couldn't officially change my major to Urban Ministries, I was granted permission to replace most of my youth ministry classes with urban-focused ones. During this time, Mr. Bob Smith, one of our esteemed Black faculty members, became my mentor, graciously taking me under his wing.

Additionally, I became a big brother in Moody's equivalent of the Big Brother Big Sister program. This initiative connected college students with young individuals residing in Cabrini Green. As mentioned earlier, Moody Bible

Institute was merely a few blocks east of this renowned inner-city housing project. For those familiar with the sitcom "Good Times," depicting the challenges faced by the Evans family—a Black family residing in Cabrini Green—one may recall J.J., known for his art and his catchphrase, "DY-NO-MITE!" My little brother's name was Reginald, and he lived on the ninth floor of one of the red bricked high-rises (but I'll delve into this further in a later chapter).

As I mentioned, I was in dire need of employment and aspired to secure a position as a youth pastor. Unfortunately, my applications were rejected by three white suburban churches. However, my fortune changed when I stumbled upon a part-time youth pastor position at Rogers Park Baptist Church, situated in the Rogers Park community on the north side of Chicago. I submitted my application, cautiously optimistic. To my delight, they displayed interest and invited me to attend their service, followed by an interview with the board. Their worship service reminded me of my Lutheran upbringing, with a few notable differences—several Black families attended, and they incorporated a few additional hymns into the service.

Following the service, during coffee hour in the Pine Room, I had the opportunity to meet the members of the congregation. Subsequently, I was called in for a meeting, which also served as an interview. They candidly expressed that their church was graying and dwindling in size. They believed that establishing a robust youth program would attract parents and breathe new life into the church. My task would be to create, build, and implement such a program. They also asked if I would be ok working in a culturally diverse setting as I may have some black students in my group. I had no issues with that, in fact, it put a smile on my face. They seemed to resonate with my vision and assured me they would discuss amongst themselves and pray before reaching a decision.

The church was located approximately 45 minutes from campus, entailing a half-mile walk from campus to the State Street Subway, followed by a 30-minute ride to Morse stop, and concluding with a mile-and-a-half walk to the church. I'll always remember that by the time I returned to my dorm room, there was already a message from Pastor Schackelford awaiting me, declaring, "You're hired!" I still chuckle to this day, wondering just how long they truly deliberated in prayer. Yet, this was undeniably God's plan for my next step on this extraordinary journey.

Now, let me provide you with some background about Rogers Park Baptist Church and the neighborhood itself. Originally a predominantly white and Jewish community, the influx of Black residents caused many members to relocate, severing their ties to the neighborhood. The pastor himself resided in the suburban town of Wheaton, Illinois, which entailed an hour's drive to the church. We had a part-time secretary on-site, while the pastor was present solely on Sundays and one Saturday each month for prayer.

Founded in 1891, Rogers Park Baptist Church, a majestic edifice of brick at the corner of Walcott and Greenleaf, is more than just a building; it is a testament to the passage of time and the resilience of faith. Inside, the sprawling three-story structure houses countless treasures - three stairwells, a large sanctuary, an intimate chapel, a spacious nursery, a well-equipped kitchen, numerous classrooms, and even a dedicated Ladies Parlor adorned with exquisite furniture and pictures.

The church's rich history, reflected in pictures and records dating back to the 1930s, reveals its integral role within the community. Over the years, it has served as a home to the Boy Scouts of America and witnessed numerous memorable gatherings in its ornate Ladies Room. Back in the day, on every first Sunday of the month over 500 members would gather for New Member's Welcome Lunch, feasting in the fellowship hall. The hall itself back at this time was impressive, boasting an incredible stage complete with floor lights, backdrops, and three rows of ceiling lights, but decaying from years of inactivity.

During my first years there, I often found myself walking through the quiet halls of this once-vibrant institution, pondering its past glory and visualizing its potential. The church, which had thrived like a country club until the early 1970s, had begun to show signs of major decay. By May 1994, average Sunday service attendance had dwindled to a mere 40, mostly aged 60 and above or twelve years or younger, as most of those kids were black from the community attending Sunday School.

It first started right here at Rogers Park Baptist Church where I encountered the harsh realities of racism, confronted by disgruntled white life-long members resistant to change, especially Black change. Despite this, I persisted in my mission, determined to breathe new life into the church. Soon, the church was bustling with over 200 young people every night, who were split into age-specific groups for Bible study and gym time. My Shorties were ages 10 to 15; while the older guys consisted of individuals from 16 to 25, 16 to 18 year olds made up the majority.

Every Sunday, like clockwork, an irate white member of the congregation would accost me, often over trivial matters like shoe marks on the floor. It was a stark contrast to the declarations of unity and inclusion proclaimed from the pulpit. The church prided itself on being a mixed congregation, openly welcoming all races to worship with us. However, this grand notion of multiculturalism often boiled down to superficial gestures such as featuring a special black gospel song once a month.

As my youth program began to flourish, the need for a larger, more welcoming space became evident. The long-abandoned Boy Scout Room caught my attention - a forgotten space echoing with the laughter of a bygone era. I proposed a renovation plan to include all free supplies such as paint and chairs as well as the volunteers to do the work. I know this would breathe new life into this neglected corner of the church.

The thumbs up to begin this transformation took an entire year, with every detail carefully considered. As part of the agreement, I promised to relinquish the room, should the Boy Scouts ever return. Their relics were meticulously packed away, each piece a silent testament to the past. Despite their absence for decades, a subtle undercurrent of anticipation tinged the church's atmosphere - a secret hope that the Boy Scouts might once again fill this space.

This process served as a metaphor for our own journey, simultaneously looking to the past while forging a path towards a more inclusive future. It was a small step, but a significant one, in creating a welcoming environment for all members of our vibrant and growing youth community. By the way, they never returned!

The church was transformed into a hub of activity, offering a myriad of programs for our youth throughout the week. It was even home to a basketball team and a small recording studio. Our Sunday evenings culminated with an Urban Style Worship Service, a modern interpretation of religious worship that began drawing in adults too.

As our community grew, racial tensions surfaced, revealing the darker side of the church's history. Racism reared its ugly head, particularly in a heated incident involving Elder John, whose derogatory comments left a lasting impact on my youth. The ensuing pain sharpened my understanding of racism, adding another chapter to the church's complex history.

I will never forget that one Saturday morning when Elder John walked into the gym. This incident remains etched in my memory, a stark reminder of the painful undercurrents that still existed within the church. On this particular day, the Pastor's monthly prayer meeting was moved from his office upstairs to the Pine Room, as Deacon Ken joined the usually solitary duo of the Pastor and Elder John. As the prayer session proceeded down the hall from the gym, the joyous echoes of basketball practice resonated through the corridors. Hearing this, Elder John, filled with rage, stormed into the gym and confronted the young players. His words, laced with racial venom, pierced the harmonious atmosphere: "What the hell are these damn Black kids doing in here"? I immediately came to their defense, but the damage was done, Elder John had finally exposed his heart only to confirm what I knew. He walked out only to return to prayer.

The profound ugliness of his outburst left a chilling echo, introducing me to the harsh reality of institutionalized racism in a place where love and acceptance should have been paramount. As I struggled to conceal my tears, I saw a reflection of my pain mirrored in the faces of the young men - a pain borne out of the unjust assertion that religion had a color preference and black was not it.

That traumatic incident felt like a blade piercing my heart, leaving a wound that, to this day, serves as a reminder of the unresolved racial biases that we had set out to overcome. The young men were so hurt we never gathered again on Saturday mornings.

The dichotomy was not lost on me. These symbolic actions didn't equate to the true essence of cultural equality. The love and dedication I harbored for the young people who came to our church fortified me amid these conflicting realities. Yet, I soon understood what the church truly sought when they had asked me to build a vibrant youth program - they envisioned a predominately white youth program.

This paradox served as a poignant reminder of the challenges that still lay ahead in our quest for genuine inclusion and equality. Despite these obstacles, my resolve to foster an environment that truly celebrated my black family remained undeterred.

Let me take you back to how my youth program at Rogers Park Baptist began. It was on a Friday night in May, guided by the warm-hearted Josephine Nelson. Josephine, in her early 70s and serving as the acting youth pastor, was a beacon of love and light despite her life being marred by pain and loss. From the moment she embraced me, handed me the church key, and introduced me to the vast premises, she became my biggest supporter, her faith in me unwavering. Even now, the memory of her stirs up a deep well of emotion; her inspiring spirit continues to illuminate my path. Although she was as white as me, her heart was not like the other members.

The following Friday night, I found myself alone, unlocking the church doors. As I moved through the Fellowship Hall towards the stage, the empty space echoed back at me. I flicked on the stage lights and allowed my imagination to fill the room, envisioning it in its heyday before time took its toll. The grandeur of this place surpassed even that of my high school stage, with its backdrops and floor lights, features we could only have dreamt of!

In the subsequent weeks, however, the hall remained largely empty, its echoes unheard except by me. But finally, a breakthrough: five young men walked in, their presence injecting life back into the room. Over time, this number grew from five to almost thirty. I won't shy away from admitting that I felt overwhelmed and intimidated during those early days. I found solace in the chair on the stage, watching them play ball until it was time to close.

This pattern continued for a few months, until I heard a voice within whispering, "It's time to face your fears." The following Friday, I took a leap of faith. After the winning shot was scored, I stepped onto the court and announced that it was time for Bible study. Some reacted with laughter, some called me names, but all of them walked out.

This was a defining moment, a stark reality check. But it was also an opportunity to confront my fears head-on, especially if I was to remain.

My efforts to include Bible study wasn't initially meet with enthusiasm, and I faced rejection, but I persevered. Week after week for nearly three months I waited in an empty gym, often in tears, questioning my calling. But each time I was close to surrendering, divine providence reminded me not to give up. Eventually, a few young men returned, and they stayed for Bible study and my outreach began to grow. By the end of my tenure, over 500 young people were regularly attending my youth program each week. How I could have used some help! But I did the best I could.

As time whirled by, my two-and-a-half years at Moody were drawing to a close. My impending graduation day stirred a dual responsibility in me: the search for a worthy successor for my church role, and the contemplation of my own forthcoming path. Yet, every opportunity seemingly extended by human hands was swiftly sealed shut by divine intervention.

For example, the summer of 1995, just before entering my senior year at Moody, I was invited back to co-direct another Camp Adventure Summer Camp for U.S. military children. This time, I would be stationed at Hickam Air Force Base in Honolulu, Hawaii. As this was the inaugural year for the camp, we received several visits from executive leadership to ensure that our work met the base's expectations. Mr. Edginton, the camp's founder, stopped by for a meeting with the Commander.

During his last visit he made it known how he was impressed by my work and offered me a full scholarship to pursue my Master's in Education, and asked me to oversee a team creating a camp for teenagers. I would then travel with him during the summers to supervise the various teen camps around the world. Without a moment's hesitation, I accepted.

Then about two weeks before I was set to leave the island, I was approached by the Director of the Youth Center on Hickam AFB. He offered me a full-time position to create a year-round youth program. For a moment, I regretted my decision to accept Mr. Edginton's offer, but I couldn't renege on my word, nor did I feel called to leave Moody. So, albeit with some regret, I declined his offer.

My senior year was punctuated by several trips to Cedar Falls, Iowa, to meet with Mr. Edginton to secure my position while finding a place to rent after graduation. However, when God has a plan for you, our plans seldom materialize as we anticipate. After several setbacks, it became clear that my path lay in Chicago, in Rogers Park, where I was cultivating a vibrant community at the Rogers Park Baptist Church. So upon graduation, I remained in Chicago, searching for full-time employment while juggling the church responsibilities.

God faithfully delivered on His promise of provision as I found myself immersed in a range of full-time roles, from working with youth at a boys' home, serving as a case manager for mentally ill adults, to becoming the Director of Youth Arts and Recreational Services for the Jane Addams Center, and even creating an after-school initiative known as Youth With A Purpose. On the side, I also picked up a part-time job at Sullivan High School, a local high school attended by many community youth. I believed this would facilitate establishing strong bonds with students and staff alike.

Juggling a full-time job, volunteering several hours a week at Cook County Jail and the Juvenile Detention Center, and orchestrating nightly activities on Tuesdays, Wednesdays, Thursdays, and all day Sundays at the church began to exact a considerable toll on me. Late at night, after dropping off the youth and spending nearly an hour scouring for a parking spot, exhaustion would often overwhelm me. Many times, unable to make the near half-mile trek to my apartment, I'd sleep in my car until about 2 am, then drag myself home for a few more hours of rest before beginning another day.

A ray of hope pierced through this demanding schedule when God led me to the Navigators in the summer of 2002. The Navigators is a globally recognized para-church organization, committed to dispatching missionaries worldwide. Under their guidance, I could raise the necessary support to commit to my church ministry full-time, eliminating the need for an additional jobs outside the church. The thrill that coursed through me upon receiving my acceptance call was immeasurable.

My new endeavor had the full backing of the church, given that the Navigators are widely respected within the white evangelical community. That fall of 2002, I was scheduled to attend a two-week orientation in Colorado Springs, the headquarters of the organization. Pastor, expressing his enthusiasm, prayed that my time of reflection in the serene mountains of Colorado Springs would kindle in me a deeper vision and mission, enabling me to return with renewed vigor and purpose.

Prior to that service while Pastor and I were talking, he asked me for a few minutes after service to meet with Jim and Jony regarding their grand daughter. It was at that moment I recalled Brother Love's call to me that morning before I left the apartment for church. "Revy D, God showed me you would be called into an emergency meeting where they would accused you of various wrongdoings". Despite my initial confusion and disbelief, his words came to pass. Following a lengthy and accusatory meeting, the pastor concluded by saying that my future as a youth pastor would be determined during my absence. I was never given an opportunity to speak.

Following this brutal experience, during my orientation time in Colorado Springs, I spent a great deal of time reflecting and praying. It became increasingly clear that my time at the church was ending. Once I returned home, I penned my resignation letter and arranged a meeting with the pastor. Through all of life's uncertainties and the unknowns that lay ahead, one thing remained a constant – my unwavering faith and the certainty that God's plan for me was unfolding exactly as it should.

Pastor was a counselor at Moody, so our meeting took place at his office. The news he shared as I settled into my seat took me by surprise. Pastor was planning to retire from both Moody and the church, and they were in the process of finding a new pastor. "Brother Dana, we're eager to hear how God spoke to you up in the mountains! We've decided to offer you the pastor's position. So, tell me, what did God reveal to you up there?" He was taken aback, and tears welled up in his eyes when I handed him my letter of resignation.

During my retreat in the mountains, it came to light that the myriad lies and accusations against me were orchestrated by a Moody student who coveted the pastor's position and saw me as the only obstacle. The young lady who had alleged exclusion had conveniently omitted the fact that I had discovered her on several occasions in a classroom on the third floor, engaged in activities that could lead to pregnancy. The condition for her return was a meeting involving her parents and me. Yet, God used this challenging situation to steer my path towards the west side of Chicago.

The devastating power of a lie cannot be overstated, as demonstrated by the infamous Rosewood Massacre. This racially charged slaughter, which led to the destruction of an entire black town, occurred in the first week of January 1923 in rural Levy County, Florida. Officially, the death toll stood at six black individuals and two white ones, but eyewitness accounts suggested a much grimmer figure, ranging from 27 to possibly 150. Contemporary news reports referred to the horrific event as a race riot. It's important to note that Florida had an alarmingly high incidence of lynching black men in the years leading up to the massacre, with one case in December 1922 gaining particular notoriety.

Before this atrocity, Rosewood had been a tranquil, predominantly black, self-sufficient town along the Seaboard Air Line Railway. Trouble brewed when white men from several neighboring towns lynched a black resident of Rosewood, following accusations that a white woman from the nearby town of Sumner had been assaulted by a black wanderer. This sparked a frenzied mob of several hundred whites to scour the countryside, hunting for black people, and nearly every structure in Rosewood was reduced to ashes.

Survivors from the town sought refuge in the nearby swamps for several days until they were safely evacuated to larger towns by train and car. No arrests were made for the atrocities committed in Rosewood. The town was abandoned by its former black and white residents, none of whom ever returned, resulting in the town's complete dissolution. The most chilling revelation came later: the white woman at the center of the incident had lied. Her assailant was, in fact, a white man.

A few days following my resignation, amidst the uncertainty of my next step, I received a call from a man named

Fletch. He told me, "I've been hearing about you. I have a three-bedroom apartment in a building I own on the west side. It's available for you to live in, free of charge. God has led you here." The subsequent months were spent wrapping up nearly a decade's worth of work in Rogers Park. Saying farewell to everything I had built was challenging, but I've always believed in obeying God's command when he instructs me to move or do anything!

So what led to the downfall of this once-thriving church? The key lies in the phenomenon known as "The Great White Flight" syndrome. As I've mentioned earlier, white residents began departing as black individuals moved into the community. Unfortunately, the white leadership of the church was either incapable or unwilling to adapt to the social and cultural transitions within the neighborhood, thus playing a significant role in the church's decline. Unfortanelty, this church is not the only church or organization or community or city or business that operates this way.

Nevertheless, my tenure from 1994 to 2002 at Rogers Park Baptist Church remains a crucial chapter in my journey of faith, resilience, and personal evolution. The day I departed was the day the church regressed to its state in 1994. The incoming white pastor declared to the congregation, "We will not continue the youth program as the previous youth pastor had established here"!

Throughout the years, despite the myriad obstacles and trials, my faith remained steadfast. This often led others to label me as obstinate or misguided. Yet, I've always felt that I had limited alternatives. God has consistently guided me, diverting me from paths not intended for me. Throughout this journey, it was only my mother who has been a constant presence, bearing witness to every twist and turn. Her faithfulness mirrors that of Mary in Luke 2:19 who, after witnessing the miraculous events surrounding Jesus's birth, treasured them in her heart. Just as Mary did, my mother has safeguarded every memory of my journey in her heart!

I warned you from the outset to prepare yourself for this journey! My life underwent a significant transformation during the years I was privileged to mentor the young men I met. These exceptional individuals, led into my life by God, became my instructors. In them, I observed raw persever-ance, resilience, and an unwavering loyalty. They contributed significantly to my growth, molding me into a better person. My heart is eternally grateful to each of them. Thank you, guys! I truly love you!

THE IMPACT OF KEYS

I hope my preceding stories have painted a vivid image of the initial 20 years of my life before my move to Chicago. I've also given a brief overview of my first near-decade in the city. Now, I'd like to delve into some specific experiences God guided me through during these initial 10 years, particularly in coming to terms with the harsh reality of racism.

As a student at Moody, I would commute via subway to the Morse stop, then walk down Morse Avenue to reach the church. Above the then 31 Flavors Ice Cream Shop, there was an apartment that caught my attention due to its prime location on Morse Avenue. As I've stated before, God shut every door leading me away from Chicago. Conversely, when my requests aligned with His plan for me to stay, they were miraculously granted. That apartment was one of such requests. Being right on the front lines with gangs just outside my doorstep, it was an ideal location for me. I signed the lease and moved in post-graduation, in August of 1996.

Quickly, I came to realize that I'd moved into a building managed by a slum lord. The apartment was a massive studio, boasting a sunroom, a spacious living room with a fireplace flanked by built-ins, much like many old Chicago buildings, and a sizeable dining room with a walk-in closet which I optimistically transformed into my bedroom. The kitchen, however, left much to be desired. Now, before you grow too envious, it wasn't without its drawbacks. The walls bore numerous holes I masked with pictures and duct tape. The apartment was infested with cockroaches and mice. My windows barely held together under years of clear tape. Nonetheless, I made it my home, and the rent was a mere $350 a month!

By this time, I had garnered a tight-knit group of 20 guys. Joe was one of them. At just 15, he had already been expelled from several schools. His parents, both struggling with drug addiction, left Joe susceptible and understandably bitter towards the world. Despite his circumstances, Joe started visiting the church and we quickly established a strong relationship that persists to this day!

I was confronted with adversities both within and outside the church. Over a two year span my car was broken into no less than 12 times. The gun violence that surrounded me also took its toll, as life here was starkly different from southern Minnesota.

One Sunday afternoon, I was invited for a home-cooked meal by my dear friends, Doug and Heather. About 10 minutes into the drive, I was seized by a massive headache, the last thing I remember before my memory evaporated. I was lost, with no idea of my whereabouts or destination. Finally, I would say nearly an hour and a half later, I remember my phone ringing; Doug was on the other end terribly worried. "Where are you? Are you ok? What's going on?" I shared just a little but his main goal was trying to guide me to his place. Once there gradually my memory returned, however, Doug's wife Heather was a nurse and she was not feeling good about this situation.

That next week was marked by intense headaches, bouts of vomiting, and a pervasive sense of disorientation. Finally, that next Saturday when my insurance kicked in, Doug accompanied me to the doctor, who ordered a spinal tap and CT Scan out of concern for a potential brain aneurism or bacterial meningitis. I was cleared for meningitis, but he did notice a small spot on the back of my head. I was given an appointment for a MRI that Monday. Due to the spinal tap I was made to remain on my back for two hours before being released.

After this appointment, Doug and I decided to grab some food at an all-you-can-eat buffet, we were both hungry! While in line to pay I was overcome with nausea, which lead to repeated vomiting in the bathroom. I started feeling weak and knew something wasn't right. Maybe I was just super hungry and my body was dealing with the traumas to include the spinal tap. It took this doctor four inserts before he got what he needed. I agreed so we got our food and sat down to ear. However, things got worse and we left immediately heading back to the ER.

I could see the concern in his eyes as he pulled me towards the car, a sense of urgency gripping the air around us. My trembling hands fumbled to fasten the seat belt, but an overwhelming fatigue suddenly consumed me. My muscles surrendered their strength, causing my head and body to slump down, sinking into the seat. With each passing moment, my body seemed to shut down, leaving me gasping for breath. In that desperate moment, I turned to God, whispering a plea for strength, a plea for life itself. If He wanted me to stay, I knew I couldn't go on without His divine intervention. And as if answering my plea, Doug gently placed his hand over my mouth, searching for the faintest sign of breath. Time seemed to stand still as I felt the acceleration of speed, a rush of adrenaline coursing through my veins and Dougs.

I awoke in the Emergency Room surrounded by doctors. Doug was instructed to call my parents to come immediately. I don't recall much from that night, apart from my left side feeling weak, hinting at a potential stroke.

The next morning, a doctor presented the possibility of brain surgery, but seeing my condition stabilize, he ordered an MRI. Before I was taken away, Doug showed up with several elders from his church to pray for me. Well, the MRI came back negative - the previously observed spot had disappeared. After a few more days of observation, I was released. I spent the following weekend recuperating with Doug and Heather, who even babysat my four-month-old Rottweiler puppy. Doug and Heather are wonderful friends who hold a special place in my heart to this day!

Finally late Sunday night my puppy and I were back home after that week of hospitalization. It was good to be home. I took a few deep breaths, hug my little puppy and thanked God for bringing me through this ordeal. I fell fast asleep!

The sharp jolt of my door buzzer rudely woke me on that early Monday morning. It wasn't an unusual occurrence – my apartment was a safe haven for my youth when they found themselves in trouble or being pursued by gangs. Despite my frail health, I hastened downstairs, but found no familiar faces awaiting me. As I trudged back up to my apartment, an uneasy feeling gnawed at my spirit, but with everything else happening, I brushed it aside.

My job as a case manager working with mentally ill adults wasn't far away, and I felt compelled to stretch my legs and say hello to my colleagues since I was up now and despite not being cleared to work for another week. After walking my puppy, Umoja, I left her in the crate and set off.

Nothing could have prepared me for the scene that greeted me when I returned home just couple hours later. My heart clenched as I saw the open crate, empty of Umoja, broken glass littering the kitchen floor, and my back door unhinged from being kicked in. My mind started to spin.

Andre, my next-door neighbor walked in, tears streaming down his face, uttering apologies. Despite being a formidable figure, much like John Coffey from "The Green Mile," Andre was a gentle giant. He had taken it upon himself to look after me, and he felt he had failed when he couldn't prevent the break-in or rescue Umoja.

Just as I was grappling with this whirlwind of emotions, the door buzzer sounded again. This time it was the police, but they were not there to help me - they had a warrant for my arrest on a supposedly missed court date for disorderly conduct while drunk. Thankfully, one of the officers recognized me through the local alderman and intervened, sparing me a trip to the police station and maybe Cook County Jail!

Left alone in my violated apartment, I sank next to Umoja's empty crate, my heart shattering as the reality of the break-in and Umoja's absence sank in. Amid the whirlpool of despair and tears, I phoned my mom. I told her, with a voice choked with emotion, "God is telling me it's time to go." I can still hear her pleading with me, "Next time they are going to come and take you, you need to come home." I hung up and sat on the floor as what do I do now.

However, the door opened moments later, and Joe walked in. His words pierced through my resolve. "Yeah, we all heard what happened and I know you going to leave us now too, just like everybody else when things get tough." His anger and disappointment were tangible when he threw his set of keys hitting me in the head. The pain in his words resonated with me, stirring the same ache I felt when I first experienced those three words "Welcome to racism". He slammed the door and walked out. I called my mom back, "Mom, God's not asking me to leave, it's the devil wanting me to go, I gotta stay."

The next day, two individuals were arrested for breaking into my apartment. The States Attorney's office recommended I move or stay elsewhere until things were settled. Thankfully, I was able to secure a new lease and had the help of 25 youth to pack up and move me within two days, down the street a few blocks as I was determined to stay in this community and fight for the lives of those God was placing in my path. I would remind myself, what if Jesus decided to stay in heaven and commute back and forth instead of enduring the hardships he faced, on account of us!

These events changed me profoundly. The experiences were a lesson in understanding racism, and more importantly, choosing to stand firm in the face of adversity. These trials tested my faith and commitment to serving my community, forcing me to choose between the comfort of my old life or bearing the cross and staying to help. By God's grace, I chose to stay and to carry the cross, for I had surrendered my life to Him.

The events also exposed the true faces of those who lived around me. Dan, who was my neighbor, and his girlfriend, who lived just below me, had been plotting the break-in for months. Both Dan and his girlfriend were white, while the two arrested individuals, James and Charles, were mixed - white and Mexican. I smiled every time I received a call from a fellow white evangelical acquaintance from back home; "See black people don't want to better themselves, you trying to help, they trying to rob and kill you"! It was a bitter irony that a situation that had been initially twisted to fit a racist narrative was the result of a more complex interplay of individuals and circumstances and the true racists hearts of those around me.

The incident propelled my ministry and outreach efforts. It was as if this ordeal was a test from God, verifying if I could handle the responsibility of ministering to some of the most wounded and broken souls. It made me ponder: Was I willing to count the cost? Indeed, I was, indeed I still am!

LIKE NEHEMIAH

This book could never encompass all the experiences and stories I've collected during my nearly 30 years in Chicago. However, I'll share a few significant lessons that I believe could serve as the foundation for transformation—provided that transformation is truly desired in one's heart. Scripture reminds us that we cannot claim to love God, whom we've never seen, while harboring hate for our Black brothers and sisters whom we see, touch, and feel every day.

I contend that all of us, as white people, are raised within the confines of racism. When the lifeblood of this nation is white supremacy, privileging whiteness, how could it be otherwise? Even now, layers of my own biases are being peeled away as God guides me deeper into understanding the depth of my whiteness, acknowledgment, and repentance, and let me add, stand against!

This process solidified my commitment to God and the work of fighting for my Black brothers and sisters until this nation sincerely acknowledges, repents, and makes amends for the damages inflicted over 400 years on a beautiful people who when they built their own, we stepped in and destroyed it over and over again and now today they only asking for equality, nothing else!

Letting go of the life of ministry I had planned with God was neither simple nor easy. The rollercoaster of emotions I experienced in the aftermath of my decision lasted for months. It would have been easier to retreat to the comfort of my first 20 years of life, a time when I didn't know a single Black person personally. Yet, the pain of five young men and the closing of every other opportunity led me to surrender my aspirations, dreams, and life to this cause. The example of Nehemiah became the cornerstone of my commitment.

The Book of Nehemiah guided me, and I now invite you to walk through it with me. I know we are not very far into my book, but it's a great time to already begin to examine your heart. Chapter one reveals Nehemiah's heartache over the plight of his people, leading him to mourn, fast, and pray before God. He confessed not only his own sins but also those of his ancestors against God.

It goes on to say in chapter one verse 3: They said to me, "Those who survived the exile and are back in the province are in great trouble and disgrace. The wall of Jerusalem is broken down, and its gates have been burned with fire." 4 When I heard these things, I sat down and wept. For some days I mourned and fasted and prayed before the God of heaven. 5 Then I said: "Lord, the God of heaven, the great and awesome God, who keeps his covenant of love with those who love him and keep his commandments, 6 let your ear be attentive and your eyes open to hear the prayer your servant is praying before you day and night for your servants, the people of Israel. I confess the sins we Israelites, including myself and my father's family, have committed against you. 7 We have acted very wickedly toward you. We have not obeyed the commands, decrees and laws you gave your servant Moses.

In a similar vein, I've witnessed the effects of the hate and injustice white America has subjected our Black family to, forcing them to grapple with the shame we've thrust upon them. The destruction of slavery, to the physical destruction of Black Wall Street and Rosewood, the Atlanta Massacre, the deliberate placement of drugs in Black communities, the unjust policing, judicial system, correctional system—all are reminders of how we have systematically dismantled their defenses and deepened their suffering. This Christian nation has never treated our black family as family!

Upon reading Nehemiah's prayer, I was moved to tears, and like him, I confessed the sins of white America, including myself and my family, we have done against our Black family and ultimately unto God. I acknowledged our wickedness and our failure to obey Christ's commandment to love God wholeheartedly and our Black brethren as ourselves.

I realized that I needed to accept responsibility not only for my actions but also for the iniquities of my forefathers spanning over 400 years. Nehemiah, born in captivity, didn't participate in his ancestors' disobedience, yet he sought God's forgiveness, acknowledging his people's collective debt. This repentance was a necessary step toward making amends, both in God's eyes and in the lives of those who have suffered unjustly—in this case, our Black family.

I understand most of my white family will disagree with me, believing that slavery is a thing of the past and refuse to accept the fact they benefited from slavery while our black family suffered from it. So I urge you to keep reading, for the purpose of my book is to uncover the truth as someone who lived for 30 years on the other side of the tracks. Only those with a more impressive resume than mine may have the authority to question not only me but also our black brothers and sisters who experience the daily impact of white privilege, regardless of their achievements or economic status. Racism transcends through all walks of life, and it is crucial that we confront this reality head-on.

Here is a scripture that none of us can escape. Our black brothers and sisters have tirelessly tried to convey the reality of injustice and racism that still persists. The issue lies with us, white America, as we have shown a lack of concern and have often chosen to ignore their voices, even going so far as to silence them. However, let me remind you of the words of Jesus.

Matthew 5:23-24 tells us, "So if you are presenting a sacrifice at the altar in the Temple and you suddenly remember that someone has something against you, leave your sacrifice there at the altar. Go and be reconciled to that person. Then come and offer your sacrifice to God."

Let me emphasize once again that we, as white individuals (especially Christians), have failed and adamantly refused to listen to the grievances of our Black brothers and sisters. We have failed to acknowledge and address the deep-rooted racism and injustices they have endured at our hands. We have disregarded their calls for equality and have actively sought to undermine their achievements. We have neglected our obligation to make amends for the harm we have caused. Therefore, be aware that the offerings you bring to God's altar may be rejected, and soon, this may even include your prayers.

To my fellow white readers, I pray that you will have the humility to recognize the harm we have inflicted and the harm we continue to perpetuate. Our Black family members have not been freely granted their rights and freedoms; they have fought and sacrificed for every ounce of progress they have achieved and yet the white Church has done nothing!

MY WHITE PRIVILEGE NEARLY KILLED ME

In the midst of my studies at Moody, after my life-altering incident that Sunday afternoon returning from church and my spiritual transformation, I knew my purpose and calling. This stirred in me a desire to learn all I could so I joined the Urban Ministry Group to collaborate with kindred spirits. I stepped into a mentoring role in Moody's Big Brother Big Sister program, linking Moody students with youth from Cabrini Green's housing project. Here, I found myself paired with a fourth-grader named Reginald, who soon became my 'little brother'.

Growing up, I was enamored with the TV show "Good Times"; I believe I've watched every episode. But I never anticipated that one day, I would find myself in Cabrini Green, the setting of the show. Perhaps God used this show as a preparation tool? Yet, in all honesty, no amount of preparation could have truly readied me for the realities I witnessed in Cabrini Green.

The fictional Evans family lived at 921 North Gilbert Avenue, Apartment 17C. Reggie resided in the Cabrini Green section known as "The Reds". He was on the 12th floor, a fact I remember vividly, given that the elevator rarely worked. The ascent up those stairs was an experience in itself, with sights and smells along the way that could easily traumatize anyone unfamiliar with such living conditions yet I could not help but think of those who lived here having to endure this day after day! Even riding in the elevator was an experience, not knowing when the last time it was serviced or checked.

Throughout my time in Cabrini, each Spring brought violent gang wars, battles for territorial dominance over various areas and buildings. The police department would notify us of this and once the violence had ceased giving us the green light to return. One year, this period of turmoil persisted for nearly four weeks. I could hardly fathom growing up amidst such conditions.

Adjacent to Reggie's building was what one might call a park. On one poignant day, we found ourselves seated on a swing, rocking gently back and forth. Reggie opened up about a summer memory from his 2nd grade; he and his best friend were swinging high when a gunshot echoed, that bullet founds its home in his best friend's head leaving a blood stain on Reggie's clothing and a trauma stain in his soul. The graphic details of that tragic day still linger in my mind.

As a white man raised in rural southern Minnesota, I was taught only where I shouldn't go—into a ghetto. I never had to grapple with the repercussions of my skin color, depending on my whereabouts or company. I was aware of the communities on the "other side of the tracks", yet never viewed my skin color as a disadvantage.

It had been weeks since I had seen Reginald and their phone was stayed on disconnect. One Saturday afternoon I was surprised when I picked up my dorm room phone and heard Reggie on the other end, a rarity given his family's persistent phone disconnection. "Dana, you think you can come get me, it's been a long time, and you'd be okay now." Taking note of his number, I quickly donned my coat and set off to meet him.

Entering Reggie's building involved ascending a flight of 8-10 steps to a concrete landing. Halfway up, a voice called out, "Hey man, where you going? Hey, Hey man!" I pressed on, only to hear the voice grow louder and closer. "Hey man, who are you man?" I replied, "I'm from Moody, coming to get my little brother," with an implicit plea for the questioner to respect my intent. The response I got was far from understanding.

Supposedly, building entry was controlled by a security guard within a bulletproof booth. But my experience quickly showed that gangs held the real power here. Upon one of the doors swinging open, I stepped inside only to be met by several men, one pressing a gun to my head and demanding to know my identity.

"I'm a Moody student, here to pick up my little brother, Reginald," I stated, heart pounding. At their command the security guard brought out a phone where I was told to call Reggie down, grateful that I had remembered his number. God had truly come to my rescue helping me remember that number only after hearing it once and writing it down on a sticky note still sticking to my desk in my dorm room. Upon seeing Reggie, the men allowed us to proceed.

It was a joy to see Reggie, but my thoughts were consumed by my earlier encounter. I felt both shame and conviction about my dismissive attitude, arrogance, and lack of respect towards those men. I had intruded upon their space, offering no explanation of my presence or intentions, a clear disregard for basic courtesy. I also failed to understand that those who patrolled the building varied. Reggie later told me that the Vice Lords were currently controlling his building, explaining why the faces were new and unfamiliar to me.

Being white, I was never educated about the constraints my skin color could impose. I never appreciated the privileges I possessed as a white man and in fact was oblivious to them. That night, after dropping Reggie off, I sought out the men I had met and disrespected earlier, apologizing for my rudeness and the audacity I had to walk into their yard as if I owned it. I asked for their forgiveness and their permission to visit again. As we shook hands, I felt a renewed sense of respect between us and was always greeted with a welcome until they too were replaced by yet another.

That day imparted a powerful lesson about my complicity in the pervasive issue of white privilege that overshadows our black family in this nation. From that moment on, I committed to asking God to reveal and help me eliminate the numerous layers of white privilege within me. Much like peeling an onion, only it's not my eyes that tear up in pain, but those of my beloved black community. I have also asked God to help me use my privilege for good until we see genuine change in our society.

A ROCK IN MY SHOE

In the bustling of people on Morse Avenue, my self-appointed mission was discreet. My prayer walk would take me down Morse Avenue in a loop, starting from the train station up to Lunt. On those warm Chicago days, I was just another face in the crowd; nothing about my attire suggested I was a pastor, I carried no bible, and my prayers were unvoiced.

As I walked, I contemplated a promise from the book of Joshua: "Every place that the sole of your foot shall tread upon, that have I given unto you." This wasn't about me claiming land for a new church building, but rather a spiritual promise of hope to those shrouded in despair, living lives that felt devoid of possibilities. My fervent prayer was for these young men to be shielded from prison and death, long enough for God's love to reach their hearts and transform their lives and open new doors of opportunity once hope begins to have its way.

Over time, trust and respect were cultivated between myself and the guys on the street. Morse Avenue was controlled by a small gang called "The Farwell Boys". They would subtly signal to me when drug business was being conducted, indicating their desire to shield me from their activities and any negative consequences that could arrive. I was also privileged to be trusted with their real names, and touched when one remarked, "Look Rev, if I ever get locked up, you got my name now so you can come visit me."

One day, following a tense exchange, I remember telling Q-Tip, "I hate seeing you sell drugs. I just wish you'd stop before you get locked up." Before I could react, he seized the collar of my shirt, pushing me against the brick wall. "You wanna see why I do this, Rev?" he challenged. "You folks from the church keep telling us to stop but never care to see why we do or help us."

Another one of my grievances, or shall we say, sources of frustration, lay in the actions of many white pastors and white Christian men who would eagerly flock to the correctional system, jails, and prisons to bring the hope of the Gospel of Jesus Christ to the black men behind bars. Yet, curiously, you would never see them on the streets or in the black communities, actively working to prevent individuals from ending up in those very same institutions. It seemed as though their involvement was driven more by the desire to feel good about themselves, to have a defense against accusations of racism, rather than a genuine commitment to address the systemic issues that lead to incarceration. They found comfort and security in the presence of officers, relying on them to shield them from the perceived dangers of the black man in the outside world.

So Q-Tip ushered me into his apartment. My eyes were immediately drawn to a tiny figure in a high chair and a little girl running towards us. A woman sprawled on the sofa, presumably from drugs, judging by the paraphernalia scattered on the coffee table. Q-Tip opened the fridge, revealing its hollow emptiness, save for some milk and baby formula. "When you can fill this," he said, gesturing to the empty fridge, "then I'll quit. But until then, don't tell me what I need to do to feed my little brother and sister."

My prayer walks weren't just for the guys. They were for me to learn, listen and hear their cries, their hurdles, and their pain. It was through these walks that we launched Godly Street Talk at a local coffee shop, a beacon of hope amidst tears and love.

Every Thursday night, I took a quiet coffee shop and transformed it into a sanctuary, a haven for conversation, a time for "Godly Street Talk". We congregated there, immersed in profound discussions about the pressing challenges these young men faced. Time and time again, their gratitude echoed through the coffee-scented air, "See Rev, you brought the church to us!" Their words, laced with gratitude and hope, were like a balm to my soul.

In the poignant quietude that marked the end of each gathering, we formed a circle. There was an unspoken agreement, a willingness, to bridge the gap between us physically as well as spiritually. Standing there, their hands clasped tightly, we prayed - for safety, for promising futures, for favorable court dates, and against impending prison sentences. The emotional intensity of these moments was palpable; it reverberated in our shared space, wrapping us in its raw, unfiltered fervor.

I became privy to their deepest secrets, their unuttered pains, their concealed shame, and the bleak tragedies that shadowed their lives. But amidst all this, one thing shone brightly - their unyielding resilience. Their refusal to surrender to despair was inspirational. These interactions, deeply moving and infinitely enlightening, taught me invaluable lessons. Indeed, I've often thought that I learned far more from those who crossed my path over these years than they could have possibly learned from me.

During one of my prayer walks, an excruciating pain, sharp as a knife's edge, shot up from the sole of my left foot to my hip. It struck with such vehemence that I was instantly brought to a halt. Carefully, I tried to step again, feeling what seemed like a mischievous stone that had wormed its way into my shoe. I removed my shoe right there, expecting the culprit to fall out. Yet, astonishingly, there was no stone to be seen. I muttered under my breath, "It must be in my sock then." As I limped the few blocks home, each step was a grimace, with the sole intention of removing that pesky intruder from my sock. However, after much scrutiny, I found no stone in either my shoe or sock. The source of my suffering lay within my own foot!

In search of relief, I found Dr. Fox, a reputed savant in podiatry. His diagnosis was swift and grim. I had a condition called Plantar Fibromas, a tumor forming on the plantar fascia muscle of the foot, a band of fibrous tissue connecting the toes to the heel bone. Surgery was the only viable solution, albeit with a significant recovery period.

With resolute courage, I underwent the operation, only to return to the streets as soon as I could, despite my doctor's strict orders of rest. My responsibilities towards the youth program and my weekly visits to Mike at the Cook County Jail, and the Juvenile Detention Center were far too significant to be put on hold. Not to mention, my two Rottweilers needed their walks! Against all odds, I would drag myself down on my butt four flights of stairs, then painstakingly crawl my way back up, two times a day. I was grateful for when the guys like Narcell would stop by to help. Navigating life on crutches and a pair of boisterous dogs was a challenge that nearly got the better of me!

Just as the prospect of liberation from both the crutches and now the cumbersome boot was dawning, a familiar pain began to torment my other foot. A subsequent visit to Dr. Fox confirmed my worst fears - another Plantar Fibroma. The cycle repeated, bringing with it crutches, boots, and the struggles of solitude.

Just as I was preparing for freedom from the second boot, I was assailed by a third Plantar Fibroma, this time in a different location. What followed was a maddening sequence of operations and recoveries, five in total. The worst blow came when I was informed that the latest tumor would require a cut through the sole of my foot, bringing with it a plethora of potential complications.

In the midst of all this, an acute appendix attack from my freshman year decided to resurface again late one night. Despite the excruciating pain, I chose not to call 911 - an act of misguided pride. Bob and Pat came that early one in the morning to drive me to the emergency room. So here I was, scooting down the steps with not only a healing foot, but now a paining appendix, and let me say, it was painful! After waiting in the ER for hours, I was finally taken into surgery. As luck would have it, Dr. Fox walked into the room where I was being peeped for surgery and immediately took charge. He set me up with his friend whom he trusted concerning my issue. Despite my appendix bursting during the operation, I made it through but remained in the hospital for four days, perhaps a divine intervention forcing me to rest.

Despite the numerous challenges I faced, my spirit remained resilient and undeterred. I persevered in my visits to Mike at Division 10, capturing the attention of Superintendent Colliers. I made it my utmost priority to fulfill God's calling for me without missing a beat. Recognizing my dedication, Superintendent Colliers called me into his office and expressed his appreciation for my commitment to Mike and the other inmates. He acknowledged the importance of individuals like me whom he and the men could trust. In a gesture of trust and collaboration, he granted me full volunteer access to his division, opening the door for me to provide assistance and support to Mike and his guys.

When I finally freed myself from the 5ᵗʰ boot, it was like breaking shackles. The freedom to walk without crutches, a boot, and with significantly less pain was exhilarating. However, after a few weeks, I found myself stumbling over my left foot, as if the muscles were failing me. My next check-up revealed the need for yet another surgery, this one more complicated and time-consuming.

Two surgeries, a week apart, left me with scars on the top of my foot and down my ankle, akin to the battle wounds of a war veteran. This time, the pain demanded obedience, and I found myself confined to my house. Yet, I had bills to pay and work to do. But like many other stories I have shared, God continued to provide for my needs.

Around two months into my tenure as Summer Camp Director at the Jane Addams Center in Chicago, my boss was fired, and I was offered her position. However, this promotion came with a harrowing ordeal of its own. The Center Director began to treat me with hostility and disrespect. Young and scared, I endured his abusive behavior for a year. The situation escalated when he denied me time off for my grandparents' 50ᵗʰ Wedding Anniversary. My grandmother and I cried over the phone. This new struggle seemed a cruel addition to the relentless cycle of physical challenges I was already fighting.

One day, the persistently abrasive voice of my boss on the other end of the phone finally pushed me beyond fear of losing my job. His message was crude and disrespectful, an undeniable culmination of the abuses I had endured. Yet, this incident was a turning point. Armed with a recorded tape of his tirade, I immediately reached out to Cheryl, the Vice President, requesting an emergency meeting. With tears in her eyes and empathy in her heart, Cheryl listened to my stories and the damning evidence on the cassette. Reassured of my safety by the President, I was offered two months of paid leave to recuperate from the incessant cycle of operations and recoveries, and, equally importantly, from the emotional scars left by the hostile environment.

I returned to my office and was visited by Stephen, the boss. The next half-hour unfolded with unanticipated candor, as he tearfully sought solace in my company and faith. He requested my prayers for an impending meeting with the top executives. So, we prayed, and that was the last time I saw him at the center. The following day, police officers escorted him as he cleared out his office, banished forever from the Jane Addams property.

Indeed, life has an uncanny knack of weaving together the good and the bad, for those who love God and are called to His purpose. My two-month paid leave, coupled with four months of accrued sick leave, gave me ample time to heal properly after the last major surgery. Upon my return, I was entrusted with more responsibilities and blessed with a well-deserved pay raise.

Eight long months later, my foot was finally free, albeit in need of significant therapy. My aspirations of rejoining a co-ed volleyball team were thwarted by an all-too-familiar pain now back in my right foot. The prospect of yet another surgery was daunting, but I resolved to have it on my birthday, November 5th, a year later. Yes, now my right foot needed that same major surgery broken up into two, one week apart from each other. See, they would stop my blood flow from just above my ankle during surgery, but after two hours tissue will begin to decay. Since this was nearly a four hour surgery, it was done in two stages.

As fate would have it, I was invited to Nigeria with Bishop Rey. The opportunity coincided with the date of my planned surgery. After much contemplation, I decided to postpone my operation by three weeks and embrace the chance to visit Africa. I yearned to witness the miracles often associated with that land and, perhaps, even be the recipient of one.

During our nine-hour flight, I found myself in a profound conversation with God, seeking His divine intervention to cure my feet. I was desperate to break the cycle of surgeries and prolonged recoveries. We spent the initial days in Lagos before journeying to Benin City under armed protection. A journey outside of my comfort zone, but my companions' unwavering faith provided solace.

At Benin City, we participated in a massive revival hosted by Mama Idahosa, who had recently taken over her late husband's church and university. We stayed on the compound, and the kindness and love shown by our hosts left a deep impression on me. However, as the last day of our trip neared, my prayer for healing remained unanswered. Feeling a tinge of sadness, I confided in Bishop Rey. His fervent prayer for my faith gave me hope.

It was the final night of the revival and just like every other one we began with electrifying energy and the powerful voice of the worship team and leader echoed through the massive gathering, of over 20,000!

Finally, we made it through the city to the stage were we sat with 10 other pastors and leaders from around the globe! The music began to play, and the worship leader offered a heartfelt prayer. However, tonight there was something different in the air. Each time the worship leader was about to start singing the first song, it was if something kept holding him back. Finally, in a bold and resonant Nigerian voice, he exclaimed, "Yes, God, I hear You!" At that moment an indescribable sensation surged through my body, starting from the feet, this powerful burning energy began to rise, engulfing my legs. At the same time he turned to face me, his eyes locked onto mine; "You, you!" he declared, his gaze unwavering. "God has heard your cry, your tumors, they are gone!" The intense burning sensation continued its ascent, reaching the top of my head. Suddenly, my consciousness faded, and the next thing I knew, I found myself lying on my back on the stage. The worship continued unabated around me. Quietly, I gathered myself, adjusting my African attire, and took a seat next to Bishop.

"God has answered you, my son. You are healed!" Bishop whispered with awe in his voice. "No one even touched you! But I saw your feet lift off the ground by a good foot. He truly healed you!"

Only Bishop was aware of the tumors I had been carrying and my earnest desire for healing. As we stepped off the stage and I descended the stairs, an overwhelming rush of emotion swept over me, and tears streamed down my face. The pain and burden that had weighed heavily on my right foot had vanished completely. It was a miraculous transformation, love from my Father.

The following morning, we embarked on our journey to Port Harcourt, the final leg of our two-week expedition through Nigeria. This is where I met Pastor Chris who later came to visit me in Chicago a few times. But as we soared through the skies on the flight back home, a burning question arose within me. I couldn't help but ask God, "Why don't you perform such miracles like this in America? I witnessed countless people experiencing divine healing during my time in Nigeria."

In response, I heard the gentle voice of God whisper, "Son, when you confine me to a box, my workings are limited to that box. But when you release me, when you allow me to operate freely, I can accomplish extraordinary things beyond imagination."

MY WALK WITH RONNIE

In the early fall of 1996, I moved to Rogers Park after my graduating from Moody. The story I'm about to share happened during a walk home from Jewel Osco on Morse Avenue. Being new to the city I quickly got to experience trying to find a parking spot, not only was this a test of patience, but a waste of gas and time. On most nights, it would take 30 to 45 minutes of driving around to secure a space, which many times ended up being a half mile away. Consequently, I found myself hauling groceries for blocks – a stark contrast to my childhood, where the most I did was carry bags from the trunk of the car to the door, a mere 5 feet!

One day, as I was walking home from the grocery store, a well-dressed Black man approached me from behind. The conversation started casually and as we chatted, I revealed that I was a youth pastor at Rogers Park Baptist Church. By this time we were standing in the parking lot next to my apartment, when this man named Ronnie, began to unfold his story. He described his struggles growing up in foster care, facing abuse, battling drug addiction, and striving to be a good father and provider. His story culminated in tears as he told me about his son, Ronnie Jr., who had died from Sudden Infant Death Syndrome (SIDS). His pain was profound: "I will never forgive myself." I tried to assure him it wasn't his fault, but his mind stayed on the fact Ronnie Jr. died in his care, while sleeping in the crib.

Over the next two years I met and talked with Ronnie on several occasions. One time he even came to the church, but only if I drove him so he could crouch down in the back seat to not be seen by potential enemies. I got the chance to meet his wife and his five beautiful daughters. Like I said, he attended the church a few times and joined us several times for "Godly Street Talk".

On the morning of February 15th 1998, I encountered Ronnie unexpectedly coming from the Morse "L" Station. He looked different – dressed in a tracksuit with a hoodie shrouding his face. He was acting unusually, seemed in a rush, and his demeanor was edgy. I could only imagine what he might be dealing with after our many conversations and his honesty about some of his bad habits. A few weeks later, the news reported a horrific crime – a woman had been raped and murdered, and the perpetrator was using her stolen debit card and this seemed to be linked to a previous rape and murder. When the man's face was shown on the news, I didn't recognize him. However, his daughter did! During that school day she shared this information with her teacher who in turn shared with her administration who contacted the authorities. Upon picking her up from after school the police had arrested Ronnie and his "partner in crime", Micheal. It was then I saw the mug shot I recognized Ronnie!

The very next day marked my first encounter with Cook County Jail. A formidable structure sprawled across 96 acres and spanning eight city blocks, this labyrinthine complex housed more than 9,000 inmates daily and around 100,000 annually across its eleven divisions. A daunting prospect for a first-time visitor, to say the least. I was aiming for Division Eight, where Ronnie was held, but was initially at a loss on how to navigate the vast expanse of the institution.

After a string of queries and directions from multiple sources, I finally found my way to Division Eight. The journey was filled with several checkpoints - pat-downs, metal detectors - all of which I dutifully underwent. I reached the waiting area around 10:30 am, signed in, and settled down for an uncertain wait.

Hours trickled by, and the day gradually transitioned into evening. Around 7:30 pm, a black woman in a white uniform was preparing to end her shift when she noticed my prolonged presence. She approached me, curiosity piqued, "Sir, I couldn't help but notice that you've been sitting here all day. May I ask who you're here to visit?" I mentioned Ronnie's name.

Her eyes widened slightly in surprise. "Oh wow, today isn't even his visiting day. But let me check something for you." She disappeared for about ten minutes, then returned with a reassuring smile. "Sir, he hasn't returned from his arraignment yet. However, given that you've been waiting all day, I've made arrangements for you to see him, I am the Superintendent." This surprising turn of events promised an unexpected encounter with Ronnie.

Finally, at around 9:00pm, I was granted an in-person visit with Ronnie. During our conversation, Ronnie adamantly insisted that he alone was responsible for the crimes and made a heartfelt request. "Please, Pastor Dana," he implored, "would you visit my best friend, Michael, in Division 10? He's completely innocent, and I need you to reassure him. I'll do everything in my power to get him out. He's got no blood on his hands. Please, tell him that."

Now armed with a basic understanding of the jail's visiting procedure, I ventured to meet Michael the following week. I could tell he wasn't expecting a white guy like me to walk into the visiting room. In this compact space, there are three of us visitors in this small room separated from our respective inmates by a thick, grimy glass barrier. I took my place on a cold steel stool, endeavoring to communicate with

Michael through a series of tiny holes in the glass—simultaneously contending with the clamor of the other two conversations, not to mention the awkwardness of our unfamiliarity.

I introduced myself and conveyed Ronnie's message, after which Michael entrusted me with a return message for Ronnie. I then cautiously asked Michael if he wanted me to keep visiting. Beneath his visible anger, I could perceive a palpable sense of pain. He seemed indifferent to the visits, so I persisted. Over the course of two years, Michael and I gradually forged a bond, so much so that even my seven foot surgeries didn't deter me from visiting him.

One day, upon my arrival, as I shared briefly in a prior chapter, a guard advised me to wait for Superintendent Colliers, who wished to speak with me. I was ushered into his office. "Young man," he began, "I'm genuinely impressed by your unwavering commitment to Michael. In all my years, I've never witnessed such resilience—nothing seems to deter you, not even your crutches and all the snow you have to walk through. We need dedicated individuals like you to assist my men here in Division 10." This meeting paved the way for my nearly 18-year stint as a volunteer at Cook County Jail as many weeks I'd be up there two to three times.

Through Michael, I became involved in the Life Learning Dorm in Division 10. We were assigned Unit B on the second floor. For five months, we enriched the lives of over 75 men, offering Bible studies, anger management lessons, tutoring, and other valuable instruction intended to inspire profound transformation within their hearts and minds. Upon completing the program, we held a graduation ceremony in the gymnasium, allowing our graduates to invite family and friends to commemorate their achievement. I was deeply moved by the tears of several men who confessed, "Pastor D, this is my first-ever achievement. It feels so good! And to finally make my Mom proud..."

My engagement with these men didn't transpire within the sanctuary of a chapel. Instead, we convened in their day room—the place where they could step out of their cells to play cards, shower, watch the lone TV, or simply socialize. It was their time of "freedom." Twice a week, I would immerse myself in their world—once for a Bible study, and the other to share experiences, listen, and learn. The poignant tales of suffering and victory I heard over those years brought us together as a family. And so, I spent most holidays with my extended family on Floor 2B of Cook County Jail. We would sing, share poetry, rap, or share personal stories that uplifted our spirits. Tears were shed as we reminisced about our loved ones outside the prison walls and grappled with the bitter memories of missed opportunities and regrettable decisions.

One holiday, I was granted the chance to bring my parents along with me. Upon parking the car, my dad had a change of heart and decided not to enter. My mom was resolute. "Well, I'm going in. I'm going to meet Mike, Dana's friend, whom I've been corresponding with." Confronted with his own biases, my dad reluctantly decided to accompany us; "Well, somebody's gotta save you from those monsters"! It was quite an adventure for them—their first visit to a jail, and not just any jail, but Cook County Division 10 Maximum Security, where the most dangerous Class X felons were housed.

The inmates were thrilled at the prospect of meeting my parents, especially my mother. They prepared for their visit as if they were expecting VIPs—ironing their uniforms by laying them our flat under their mattress as they slept and ensuring they were clean-shaven as they wanted to look respectful for my parents arrival. When my parents stepped onto Floor 2B, they were treated like celebrities. For the next 30 minutes, the men showcased their talents for my parents' entertainment. The final half-hour was spent in earnest conversation. My mom sat next to Mike, while my dad was elsewhere, engrossed in his own discussions. I stood and observed the transformative power of these men's love on my parents. When Officer Carter signaled it was time to leave, I had to gently urge my dad to wrap up his conversation, a challenging task for someone as talkative as him!

The ride back from the jail was enveloped in silence. I'll never forget the sight of my father's reflection in the rearview mirror—tears streaming down his face—a testament to the profound impact these men had on him in a span of an hour. From a man who called them monsters, to a man who was shedding some tears, something I had never really seen my dad do. My mother shed her own tears for Mike and the others.

Over nearly 18 years, I spent countless hours at the jail, forming bonds with extraordinary men and nurturing my friendship with Mike, who would go on to become a respected leader on his floor. He had experienced a fair share of personal tragedy, including the loss of his mother to cancer, which led him down the path of drug abuse that led to that one fateful day, when he was arrested alongside Ronnie being implicated in a crime he hadn't committed.

During this time, I grew close to Mike's Aunt Mary. For at least five years, I would pick her up every Sunday for church, after which I'd be treated to a hearty soul meal that would last me for several days. Convinced of Mike's innocence, we enlisting the support of Professor Kling from Kent Law School as we lacked the resources to hire a lawyer for such a case as this. Fortunately, Professor Kling agreed to take his case and have his students help in presenting a strong argument against Mike being falsely accused of these crimes. Over the next six years, my eyes were opened to the many injustices faced by Black men in our justice and court systems.

We had indisputable evidence that contradicted the statement made against Mike—their own photographic evidence, no less! They concocted a role for Mike using Ronnie's confession, but when the photographs emerged, the fabrications were revealed. Regrettably, our evidence to debunk the statement and reveal the judge did not allow the police's torturous practices permitted in the courtroom. Consequently, after eight long years, Mike was found guilty and sentenced to life in prison for the one, 65 additional years for the other. The painful truth of those words, "Welcome to racism," was etching deeper and deeper into my consciousness.

Fast forward 24 years to this day in April 2023 as I write this. Mike, despite his circumstances, has earned a Master's Degree and continues to command respect as a 'Joseph' figure among his peers. We've represented Mike before the Illinois Prison Review Board, pleading with the Governor of Illinois to release this innocent man. One of the prerequisites for this is to have a financially stable caretaker. Remarkably, my parents stepped up to the plate and agreed to assume this role. Since 1999, they've been sending Mike a minimum of 100 dollars a month for commissary expenses. During most of their visits to me, we dedicate a day to visit Mike, who is now confined to a prison. On one such visit, my father promised Mike that they would go fishing together in his boat—a small gesture to fulfill one of Mike's wishes. The poignant memory brought tears to Mike's eyes when I informed him of my dad's passing. Shortly after, Aunt Mary also passed away. "Well Dana, it's just you and Mom now," Mike lamented.

Mike's case has been taken up by the Innocence Project, and we're still awaiting a response from the Governor. I talk to Mike at least one to three times a week.

As for Ronnie, he's been sentenced to spend the rest of his life behind bars. On God's instruction, I attended a few days of Ronnie's trial. On this particular day, a man around my age, 30, testified about being assaulted, beaten, and robbed by Ronnie. "One day, I was walking home when this well-dressed Black man struck up a conversation with me. As I neared the entrance to my apartment building, he brandished a gun and threatened to shoot me unless…" His story echoed the experiences of four others, with one stark difference—I was the only one left unharmed. Although Ronnie was the reason I met Mike, I couldn't harbor resentment towards him. But, it begs the question: how does one reconcile with such a complex situation? I know, what was meant for my evil, has turned out to be a blessing…Mike, and all the guys I had the honor of meeting during our "Life Learning Dorm" years! To all the guys from floor 2B who came through the "Life Learning Dorm", I thank you!

A BEAUTIFUL PAINT JOB

Over my 18-year tenure at Cook County Jail, I spent countless hours with the men of Floor 2B, even on many holidays! I saw past the standard-issue DOCC jumpsuits and hardened facades, seeing instead hearts wounded by a society that didn't just reject them, but also pushed them further into the shadows or what I call the modern day cotton fields.

Briefly, I mentioned Floor 2B or the "Life Learning Dorm," a rehabilitative program that I helped create. We were granted permission to transform these men's lives through Bible study, tutoring, counseling, and even by introducing computers for their use! The transformation was palpable. After five months, we held a graduation ceremony, inviting their families to witness their loved ones—fathers, sons, brothers, uncles, husbands, and friends—receive completion certificates. Families were even granted a few minutes to share some finger food and touch their loved ones, a contact many had been deprived of for years.

Here's a crucial side note: the magnitude of injustice I witnessed behind those walls was sufficient to expose the grim reality of our correctional system—modern-day cotton fields, if you will. Most Illinois prisons are privately owned—echoes of the past, but now in the guise of prisons. I have countless stories beyond Mike's, enough to fill another book.

Consider this: the 5th Amendment states that one is innocent until proven guilty. Then why are these men treated as criminals while awaiting trial? They are seen as guilty, charged as guilty until they are officially found guilty, but always guilty trying to prove their innocence.

Consider Jerome, accused of rape. It took nearly eight years for the State to present the required DNA evidence that then cleared his name. These men endure agonizing waiting periods of one to six months each time the State needs more time. Prolonged pre-trials wear them down, leading many to plead guilty in exchange for time served. Now bearing a lifetime mark of guilt, they just yearn for release. Even those who are "freed" are forever shackled.

Back to the main narrative: after the men graduate from the Life Learning Dorm program, we dispatch them, in groups of 10, to other floors. They become positive leaders throughout the division, helping to quell conflicts. The change in Floor 2B was evident, convincing the "powers that be" that our program worked, and spreading graduates throughout the jail reduced issues on other floors.

This Christmas, I stayed in Chicago to celebrate Christmas Eve Day with the men. Waking up that morning, I was excited for them to enjoy a meal from an outside restaurant—a huge treat in their circumstances. In those moments, I realized how we take for granted simple comforts like backed chairs, when some only have stools.

Parking in North Chicago is an ordeal, especially after 10 p.m. Many nights, I drove around for half an hour, searching for a parking spot within half a mile of my home. I'll never forget the days of learning to carry all my groceries in one trip to avoid a second trek over five blocks. When my fingers turned purple from strain, I'd set the bags down—not to leave them, but to restore blood flow to my fingertips to continue my journey!

On this Christmas Eve morning, I found my white Kia Sportage transformed into a graffiti canvas with neon blue spray paint—lines, circles, 'x's and unrepeatable words adorned my vehicle. Trying to feel better, I looked for other similarly decorated cars on the street, only to find mine was unique. My initial excitement quickly turned to sadness, confusion, and worry. Now what?

As a single man, I'd developed the knack of maintaining an excellent dialogue with myself. "Dana, there's nothing you can do now, the men are waiting, deal with this later," I told myself. So, agreeing with my own advice, I decided not to let this incident ruin my day. Despite the curious looks and comments I received driving downtown on the last shopping day before Christmas, I just smiled, thinking, "If only you knew."

Entering the jail, I was met with a sight of nearly 100 men, dressed to the nines in their pressed DOC clothes, clean-shaven and lined up, resembling Kings! Their creativity was astounding. The world has no idea how much greatness lies behind those bars. The realization that a cure for cancer, diabetes, or HIV might have been locked in the mind of an innocent inmate touched my heart. I always reminded my white congregation members that injustice affects us all as your dying loved ones from cancer could have been healed, but our injustices have him or her behind bars! I employed them to look at all the inventions given to us by our Black family we would die if we didn't have.

I spent the next several hours eating, worshiping, studying, and bonding with the men. The incident with my car faded from my mind until I exited the jail, only to be reminded of it. "Now what, Lord?" I murmured, walking towards my car. As I was about to get in, one of the Chaplains saw me and offered help. A friend of his owned a car shop, and despite it being Christmas Eve, he was willing to help.

The paint was less than 24 hours old, so with some solution and a bit of elbow grease, my car was back to normal within an hour. The shop owner's gift to me—a symbol of God's faithfulness—touched me deeply. Driving home, I fought back tears, reminding myself to stay focused amidst the hurdles life throws. A smudge of blue paint we missed in my side mirror served as a reminder of God's love and faithfulness.

Even now, I think about the thousands of men who touched and impacted my life. Their resilience and faith have shaped me, their wounds have moved me. I cherish those years and regularly read through the letters they sent me, so many that they filled a three-drawer file cabinet!

Tackling racial obstacles was indeed a struggle—their experience with my white identity, and my interaction with their black identity. Sadly, our society's deep-seated injustices often lead our young black men to two unfortunate destinations—the metaphorical cotton fields or the grave. I've had the painful responsibility of saying goodbye to more young men than I can count, but here are two of my most painful ones.

I will forever carry the weight of heartbreak, etched deeply in my memory, as I recall the tragic loss of Edward. Since he was leaving for college in the morning, his employer threw him a good-bye party. As he and several of his friends were walking home, a gang began to shoot leaving Edward dying on the sidewalk. The sorrow echoed through the community, but it was his mother who bore the brunt of the pain. I kneeled with her for an hour or more, desperately scrubbing away her son's blood from the unforgiving pavement. Her anguished cry still haunts me, "No one is going to walk on my son!"

One Sunday, Edward's mother came to church to speak with me. Her voice trembled with gratitude as she uttered words that pierced my soul, "Dana, my cancer has taken over, but I couldn't leave this earth without expressing my heartfelt thanks for all you did for Edward and me." Shortly after our conversation, she passed away, leaving behind another void in my heart.

And then there was Narcell. He had accompanied me on several trips back home, displaying unwavering dedication as he assisted in walking my dogs and caring for them. After being expelled from school, Narcell's life spiraled into unproductivity. However, he found the strength within to make a complete turnaround. He earned his GED and caught the attention of the YMCA director through his selfless acts of helping younger kids in the gym. As a result, he was offered a job that brought newfound purpose into his life. Just weeks before his marriage and the birth of his child, a phone call arrived, altering the course of my existence once again.

The images of seven bullets tearing through a human body, with one finding its mark in the head, will forever be seared into my mind seeing Narcell lay lifeless on this plastic covered hospital bed. The heart-wrenching cry of Mama Gloria echoed through my being as they took away her 20-year-old son, his vital organs destined to bring life to someone in need. Through his death, others now live on, and his daughter Brooklyn stands as a living reflection of him. In the face of this immense hardship, his family became my own. I had the solemn honor of laying Mama Gloria to rest, just as I had done for Narcell almost two decades prior when cancer prematurely stole her from our midst, leaving us all shattered and another void in my heart.

I understand that my white family may be perplexed, questioning how their behavior or racism could be responsible for the heartbreaking stories I've shared since it's black on black crime? However, I implore you to keep reading, to open your heart and seek understanding. It is through this journey that you will witness the unchecked injustices prevalent in our society - injustices in business, education, religion, and the legal system. These insidious forces relentlessly push our men towards two tragic destinations: prison or the grave.

As we delve deeper into the chapters ahead, I invite you to stand alongside me, to confront the realities that have plagued our black communities for far too long. Let us shed light on the systemic issues that perpetuate the cycle of despair and inequality. Together, we can strive for change, we can fight for justice, and we can work towards a future where hope, healing, and true equality prevail.

This is why the losses I may have endured, including my beautiful paint job, pale in comparison to the love I have developed for this community. They are not significant enough reasons for me to turn my back on the people who have captured my heart.

36 HOURS: MIKE'S STORY

I believe there is no one better suited to share his story than Mike himself. So here it is, Michael Sanders' harrowing tale of the worst 36 hours he has ever endured, an experience that continues to haunt him to this day.

Let me begin by introducing myself as Michael Sanders. This story is about my personal journey through an unimaginable nightmare that unfolded over the course of 36 agonizing hours. This is a story that completely upended my life, as I was kidnapped from my world and falsely imprisoned for the rest of my days.

It all began on March 8th, 1999, a day etched into my memory. At the time of my arrest, I was simply a passenger in my friend Ronny's car. He and his girlfriend had swung by to pick me up from work, intending to drop me off at my home after picking up their daughters from daycare.

Little did I know, as we approached the daycare center, Ronny spotted two plainclothes detectives parked in front of the building. Fearing trouble, he hastily instructed Sherlinda to continue driving. In the blink of an eye, those detectives were tailing us, and within moments, we were apprehended, less than a block away from the daycare.

A detective approached the passenger window, his gun drawn, and demanded Ronny's name. Ronny, in an attempt to protect his identity, provided an alias, as his eight-year-old daughter had inadvertently revealed his true name to the detective earlier that day.

You see, his daughter had innocently informed her teacher that she saw her father on the news. The news segment depicted Ronny allegedly attempting to access the victim's ATM card while I stood in the background, a mere observer. In that moment, reality seemed to shift into slow motion, as shock and confusion gripped me. I suddenly realized that the same detective who had Ronny at gunpoint was now aiming his weapon at me, demanding that I identify myself. Without hesitation, I provided him with my true name. Ronnie and I were then ordered out of the vehicle, handcuffed, even though I had no warrant for my arrest. But that didn't matter. We were taken to the Belmont and Devon police station first, before being transported to the infamous Area 3 station at Belmont and Western, where the Violent Crimes Homicide Division was located.

Now that I have explained the events leading up to my arrest, I will recount the grueling 36 hours that followed, the hours that forever changed my life.

Upon entering the station, I was led into a chilling room devoid of windows, shrouded in darkness. Ironically named the "Camera Room," despite the absence of any cameras to document the proceedings, it was there that I found myself shackled to a ring on the wall, sitting next to a cold steel bench. Uncertain of the horrors that lay ahead, I awaited my fate. Detective Louis, the first interrogator, wasted no time in pressing me about the murders. I firmly and repeatedly insisted, "I had nothing to do with them. I possess absolutely no information about the murders. I wasn't there!"

After a brief absence, Detective Rossi stormed into the room, a personification of malevolence. This second encounter was characterized by physical abuse and an onslaught of profanities. Together, Detectives Rossi and Louis relentlessly interrogated me, demanding answers about the murders. "I know nothing about them! I am innocent!" I fervently proclaimed. However, it was evident that Detective Rossi was dissatisfied with my response. In a violent fit of rage, he repeatedly slapped me, his punches landing on my quivering lip. "Stop lying, you damn N**er!"

Subsequently, Detectives Louis and Rossi claimed to possess DNA evidence and requested my consent to undergo a DNA test. Driven by my unwavering innocence, I willingly signed a waiver form, agreeing to the test. They swabbed my mouth and left me confined in that desolate, lightless room for agonizing hours. The passage of time seemed interminable, exacerbated by the absence of food, water, and even basic necessities like bathroom breaks.

By that point, the torment had taken its toll on my sanity. I had never endured such barbarism before. Lying on the cold steel bench, I succumbed to tears, crying myself to sleep. However, my respite was abruptly shattered by a barrage of loud voices. Detectives Louis and Rossi returned, ready to resume their relentless questioning. "I told you I don't know anything! I am innocent!" I fervently reiterated, my words falling on deaf ears.

Enraged by my response, Detective Rossi unleashed his fury upon me, striking me repeatedly in the face. "Stop lying, you N**er! You know you did it! Your accomplice Hinton spilled everything!" he bellowed. In an attempt to undermine my innocence, he questioned, "Why would Hinton provide you with money if you were not present at the murders?" Undeterred, I steadfastly maintained, "I was not there. Hinton is lying. I had no involvement whatsoever!"

Detective Louis exited the room momentarily, returning with Ronald Hinton in tow. He posed the critical question to Ronald: Was I present at the murders? Initially, Ronald hesitated, but Detective Louis, fueled by aggression, forcefully pushed him against the door frame. Finally, Ronald nodded, indicating my alleged presence. Stunned and bewildered, I stood there in a state of disbelief, silenced by the unfolding injustice.

Detectives Louis and Rossi escorted Hinton out of the room, leaving me alone in that frigid, lightless chamber, still denied basic necessities. Time ceased to have meaning as I drifted in and out of restless sleep, awakened intermittently by the echoes of racist rants that pierced through the darkness. Then, they positioned me in the center of a room teeming with 12 to 15 white officers, their expressions filled with animosity. Among them, I distinctly recall a red-haired officer with a fiery glare, who shouted directly into my face, "I am a white hillbilly boy who hates N**ers!" His words were punctuated by the physical blow of his hand striking my face and head. "We have fingerprints, you lying N**er!"

Fear consumed me, as all the officers surrounding me were white. The atmosphere exuded dominance, emphasizing the overwhelming power imbalance. Eventually, they left me alone once more in that dark, windowless, and frigid room. Every screech of dress shoes against the floor made my heart skip a beat, for it signaled the impending return of the detectives. What would they subject me to next?

Just as anxiety tightened its grip on my soul, a new figure entered the room: Lieutenant Nicklas. He inquired about the case, and I replied with unwavering conviction, "I don't know anything about it. I was not there." Sensing my vulnerability, he asked, "Do you have any children?" With a heavy heart, I responded, "Yes, I have a two-month-old daughter." He issued a chilling ultimatum, "If you want to see her again, I advise cooperation. Otherwise, a life sentence of 60-plus years awaits you. Cooperate, and you'll face charges of burglary, serving only a few years before moving on with your life."

As we conversed, Detective Louis reappeared, highlighting the supposed lesser severity of burglary compared to rape and murder. Detective Rossi followed suit, delivering two forceful slaps to my face. "Tell the fucking truth, you N**er!" he bellowed. Detective Louis proceeded to recount his version of events, repeatedly drilling the narrative into me, correcting any perceived deviations. Finally, satisfied with their coercion, Detective Louis informed A.S.A. Falagario, who later called a court reporter to document the statement. Exhausted and depleted, I received a meal from Burger King, some water, and the opportunity to use the washroom - 36 hours after the ordeal began.

In conclusion, I was framed for two murders I had no knowledge of. The police shattered my will through physical abuse, manipulated my mind through psychological coercion, and poisoned my spirit with hatred. Twenty-four long years have passed, each day a reminder of a life spent locked away as an innocent man. Yet, deep within me, hope remains. I entrust my future to God, fervently believing that He will one day set me free.

I wanted to take a moment to share with you the incredible story of my dear friend, Mike. Through his personal journey, I aim to shed light on the profound injustices that lurk behind the scenes, hidden from the reach of social media, where the true face of racism often remains obscured. Knowing Mike's story breaks my heart, and I struggle to contain the anger and resentment I feel towards the white police officers and detectives responsible for his plight, and the thousands of others we have never heard of. These wicked individuals have destroyed the lives of countless innocent black men, fueled by a sense of impunity as the consequences for their actions seem nonexistent. It is a tragic and hypocritical reality that while our nation holds others accountable for war crimes and mistreatment of prisoners, we perpetuate torture, false convictions, and even death within our own justice system.

Over the years, Mike and I have grown to become the closest of friends. We speak to each other weekly, cherishing the rare moments when he can secure extra phone time from a fellow inmate who doesn't need it. Sometimes, we're fortunate enough to have two or three conversations in a week. During one of our recent calls, I found myself falling into a heavy silence as I struggled to hold back tears.

As we reminisced about the past, I asked Mike about his initial thoughts regarding our friendship during those early visits. His response hit me like a bolt of lightning. "Truthfully? I thought you were sent to kill me. I believed the District Attorney had planted you in my life to befriend me, only to extract a confession regarding my alleged involvement in the murders. But over time, I came to realize that you were not sent to me by the DA to end my life. Instead, you were sent by God to bring me life. You are the light that shines hope in my darkest days."

While Mike often credits me with keeping his hope alive, it is he who truly inspires me and strengthens my faith. How can I worry about job security or God's provision when I witness Mike's unwavering trust in Him for his very life? Mike's resilience and unwavering spirit have fueled my determination to continue fighting against the scourge of white supremacy and the devastation it has wrought upon the lives of our black brothers and sisters.

Currently, Mike is diligently penning his story, a testament to his indomitable spirit and unwavering hope. Join me in fervently believing for Mike's release so that he may share his powerful narrative with the world beyond prison walls. We love you, Mike, and stand beside you in this fight for justice and freedom! You are a modern-day Joseph, and your story will be a beacon of light to all who hear it!

GIVEN NO VOICE

Since 1998, walking alongside Mike has been an eye-opening journey, revealing the deep-rooted injustices present from law enforcement to the judicial and correctional systems. Mike was held for 36 hours until he resignedly agreed to their pre-written confession. It was only at his arraignment that he learned the charges were far more serious than burglary, instead being accused of double pre-meditated murder and murder with a likelihood to cause harm. Thankfully, we had the support of Professor Kling from Kent Law School for Mike's first case.

This experience opened my eyes wide! We had evidence that could have exonerated Mike, proving it was impossible for him to have been involved in the murders. How could Mike leave out the back door when your pictures reveals it was still chained. Yet, Judge S. barred us from presenting this evidence contradicting Mike's so-called confession. By denying us the chance to defend Mike with the truth, the State silenced him, they took his voice away. This would have not only freed him but also exposed the pervasive injustice from the detectives upward. How can a jury accurately determine guilt if one side is denied a voice?

Mike wasn't the only one! Jermaine waited nearly eight years for the State to correctly analyze DNA evidence. He frequently returned to court only for the State to ask for more time. This tactic is distressingly effective, often breaking the resolve of the inmates, making them more inclined to accept a plea deal out of fear of receiving the maximum sentence, poorly defended by over worked public defenders. This is a common strategy when the State lacks the evidence to prove their case. I've heard it time and again, inmates resigning themselves to plea deals in the hope of an early release, fearful of the penalties they might face otherwise. Even though I've never been in their shoes, I can understand why they might make such a choice. Yet, in the end, the State wins, and these men end up with a record that may land them back in the system or at least keeps them tied to it.

The living conditions these men endure while incarcerated demonstrate their lack of voice. Although the court asserts we are "innocent until proven guilty", they're treated as guilty before their trials. Cook County Jail isn't a prison, it's a holding place primarily for individuals accused of a crime. But why are they living in conditions that dehumanize them? Why are their rights stripped away while they are still presumed innocent? Where is their voice in proclaiming their innocence?

The silencing of their voices, and the impact it has on their spirits, is unimaginable. It's enough to drive anyone to the brink of insanity. This reminded me of my own frustration as a child when my parents would make a hasty judgement without hearing both sides of the story or worse, ignoring my side!

Over the years, I've identified those officers who stood with me, and those against me, not out of personal reasons, but out of disdain for the inmates having any comfort. I've also encountered officers like Carter, who genuinely cared for the inmates and never wished to see them return. I've tried to foster peace even through small gestures like bringing donuts for them.

One morning, I arrived at the front desk after the first two shakedowns, expecting the usual greeting. Instead, I was met with silence and stern faces. Even my donuts couldn't bring out a smile. I was informed that my volunteer status had been revoked, with no reason provided. My pleas to speak with the Superintendent fell on deaf ears. Finally the guards were able to move him to come and speak with me. His hostility was palpable as he vowed to ensure I'd never be allowed back into Cook County Jail or any State Prison, and promptly dismissed me.

After bidding farewell to the guards at the front entrance and crossing 26th Street, I paused midway through the grass lawn. Turning around, I absorbed one last look at the place that had been an integral part of my life for nearly 18 years. Tears welled up in my eyes, a strange juxtaposition, as I was mourning my removal from a place everyone is crying to get out. To me, these men weren't simply inmates; they were my family.

This monumental event took place in Spring 2016, and I haven't set foot in Cook County Jail Division 10 since. During a phone call with Mike in April of 2023, he shared how my presence had made a significant impact on the guys during my time at the county. They admired me, discussing my visits even after I'd left. "They looked up to you, Dana," Mike relayed. Then, he shared a surprising revelation involving Christopher, who I remembered for his impressive sketch of my portrait.

Apparently, during a shakedown, Officer Ben found my picture among Christopher's belongings. He had forgotten to return it, and they used this as a reason to expel me which could have been easily explained, but I wasn't given a voice! Soon the whole ministry was shut down. For our black family, it is not a correctional system, it is a monetary system.

The experience illustrated a harsh truth: when you're up against a powerful system, your voice can be silenced or rendered meaningless. I was granted a glimpse, a tiny taste, of the anguish endured when our black family's voice is snatched away.

SUNNY KOOL!

I held the position of Director of Arts and Recreational services from 1997-2002 for the Jane Addams Center. During my final two years there, I became good friends with Terry, who was in charge of our teen training program. He was a powerhouse in his church, passionate about helping at-risk youth and young adults. He was a beacon of encouragement for me and taught me more than a few things.

One day, Terry approached me with a unique proposition. "Brother Dana," he began, "my older brother is getting out of prison. I think you'd be a great influence on him, and I'd like you to meet him." I was genuinely honored that Terry trusted me with such a task. So we made this meeting happen.

When I met Sonny Kool, I thought I was meeting Mr. Clean who stepped out of a TV commercial and into reality. He towered at six feet four, his biceps rivaled the size of my thighs. If I met Sonny in a dark alley, I would've run, no kidding, his presence was very impactful! But Sonny liked me, just as Terry predicted. We started hanging out on the North side streets where he used to run before his prison days. While most folks hadn't met him, the mere mention of his name rang familiar. Sonny Kool had made a name for himself back in the day when he was on those streets.

Meanwhile, a group of college students from Kentucky was volunteering in the inner city, learning about urban neighborhoods' history. Whenever I hosted volunteers, I made it a point to educate them about the inequities our underserved communities face. How our schools have a single computer lab while white suburban schools have tablets for each student. How red-lining affected our Black communities. How our neighborhoods are food deserts with expired produce shipped from suburban grocery stores. I wanted them to understand the systemic hurdles that put people in survival mode.

Sonny found it fascinating that these students, most of them white, were keen on learning about life in the inner city. He joined us, sharing invaluable insights that gave the students a lot to ponder. By the time they joined my worship service before heading back home, they had warmed up to Sonny's magnetic personality.

In the finale of our church service, my mentor and good friend, Minister Gwen, invited the congregation to step forth if they sought prayer. Sunny strode forward, tears glistening in his eyes. He whispered a plea for prayers. As he did, I took the reins of the service, providing Minister Gwen and her prayer partner the opportunity to sequester Sunny away in a modest classroom for a private conversation and prayer.

Once the last song had been sung, and the college group had been seen off, I moved to say goodbye to Minister Gwen. She grabbed my arm, her eyes urgent. "Pastor Dana, you must call me immediately once you're in your car. It's paramount!" she stressed.

My plan was to head home, freshen up, and walk my dogs before delivering Sunny back to the South Side where he was staying. I tried to call Minister Gwen several times as I was walking the dogs, but they just bounced into a void of unanswered ringing. By the time I got back to the apartment, Sunny had dozed off in the armchair. My two faithful

Rottweilers quietly padded through the room, heading for a refreshing gulp of water and a cool kitchen floor.

Sunny awoke as I entered the room, and we began a reflective discussion about the week spent with the college group. Yet, as our conversation veered towards biblical scriptures and Jesus Christ, I noticed a subtle change in Sunny's disposition. A sense of agitation began to brew within him. "Stop, Dana, I don't want to hurt you," he suddenly interjected, throwing me into a world of confusion. I had no idea what he meant. "Hurt me?" I echoed, baffled. "Yes, I don't discuss religion and bible stuff," he insisted, which struck me as odd considering his recent participation at the church service. His statement had an eerie effect, and my dogs sensed it too. Like spooked deer, they bolted from the kitchen, disappearing into my bedroom.

Hoping to ease the tension, I broached a new subject. "So, how was your meeting with Minister Gwen? Do you like her eccentric self?" I asked, trying to lighten the mood. Little did I know that I was leaping out of the frying pan and into the fire. Sunny's agitation escalated. He lowered his head, pulling at his shirt. In a sudden display of brute strength, he ripped his shirt off and rose to his feet, his eyes morphing into snake-like slits. He marched towards me, repeating his warning. Just as he was about to make contact, it was as if he had collided with an invisible glass wall. Rebounding off the unseen barrier a total of three times, he crashed back into his chair, plunging into an eerie, instant sleep.

In the face of such an uncanny event, my mind was a whirlwind of terror and disbelief. Gathering my wits about me, I fled to my bedroom, acting like a classic horror movie protagonist (white person) who chooses to hide within the murder house instead of running away. I blocked my door with a dresser for added protection. A wave of panic washed over me as I realized I was trapped on the fourth floor. Frantically, I started tying together bedsheets to form a makeshift escape rope. In the midst of my frantic efforts, a divine whisper reached me, "Greater is He who is in who?" The voice echoed until clarity dawned on me, "Greater are You who is in me!" With newfound courage, I untied the makeshift rope, shut the window, and fell into a fitful sleep.

Come morning, Sunny sat unmoving in his chair, wide awake. "I warned you to stop. I didn't want to hurt you, but I know you are of God!" he uttered, his voice bearing a strange calmness. The ride to the South Side was filled with an unsettling silence, only broken by our brief farewell. I then drove off to work.

As I walked into my office, the steady blink of my phone's message indicator signaled the arrival of unheard voicemails. This wasn't an unusual sight for a Monday morning. However, the content of the next eight messages, all from Minister Gwen, sent a shiver down my spine.

"Pastor Dana," her voice echoed in each message, tinged with panic, "I need to talk to you about Sunny. Please, your cell phone is going straight to voicemail. I've been trying to reach you." Her concern escalated in each successive message, the urgency palpable in her tone. "Oh, Pastor Dana, I pray you're still alive. Please, call me. There's a demonic presence in Sunny."

With a sense of foreboding, I dialed Minister Gwen. Her initial response was a cry of relief, "Oh, God, I feared you were gone! Oh, God!" I assured her, explaining how I had repeatedly tried to call her, only to be met by the frustrating and seemingly endless ringing that led to her voicemail.

"What happened with Sunny?" I asked, my heart pounding. Minister Gwen began to share about her chilling encounter with Sunny in that small Sunday school classroom after the church service. As she and her prayer partner,

Julia, began to speak and pray with Sunny, a horrifying event occurred.

"Julia abruptly got up and left, leaving me alone with him. I was in shock. I never let myself be alone with a man, and Julia has never abandoned me before," Gwen confessed. As she continued to pray, Sunny underwent a terrifying transformation. "He lowered his head, and when he lifted it, his eyes had morphed into the chilling slits of a serpent!"

Overwhelmed by fear, Gwen tried to escape, but the doorknob came off in her hand. She pounded on the door, her screams for help eventually answered by someone who opened it. Her voice dropped to a whisper, "I wanted to warn you, don't let him into your house. He could be lethal."

I responded to her, "Oh Minister Gwen, let me tell you about my experience last night..."

I never encountered Sunny Kool again after that evening. A chilling phone call later brought news of his death. And with it, a terrifying revelation about his past: Sunny had been imprisoned for 35 years, serving time for several murders he committed between the ages of 11 and 17. And that, dear reader, concludes the tale of my encounter with Sunny Kool.

WELCOME TO THE WEST SIDE!

Bidding farewell to Rogers Park was a tumultuous affair. Despite the adversity that led to my departure, it remained a painful transition. I've always been a man of commitment, fiercely stubborn, sometimes to my detriment. However, when Divine Guidance whispers in my ear, I know it's time to let go and follow. It was in this spirit that I found myself journeying to a new chapter in life, heading towards the infamous West Side of Chicago, North Lawndale - colloquially known as K-Town or Killer Town.

Uncertainty clouded my future. I didn't know where I would live or how I would afford rent, but this didn't deter me. But just two weeks into this decision to move, I received a phone call. His name was Fletcher, a man I had never met but was acquainted with through Jeff, a friend from the Life Learning Dorm, reached out. His backstory was fascinating.

Fletcher had a checkered past as a drug dealer in the very same community. After a personal struggle with cocaine addiction, he became homeless and nearly perished on the streets. After checking into a hospital to die, he underwent a profound transformation. By the time I met him, he was a married father of seven who owned multiple properties in North Lawndale, providing housing to those battling poverty. He often endured losses when tenants couldn't pay their rent, yet he patiently worked with them, demonstrating a profound commitment to giving back.

One of Fletcher's properties, a three-flat on Spaulding Avenue, had a vacant apartment. It was this place he offered me as a potential home, an unexpected blessing that solidified my decision to move.

The apartment required considerable care before it was habitable. It needed paint, floor refurbishment, and a significant deep cleaning. The previous occupant, struggling with obesity, had not kept the place tidy. For example, the furnace and hot water heater closet was filled with old cat litter. The family cat was intended to control a mouse problem. Even the top of the cabinets bore witness to several inches of roach droppings. Despite the grim condition, I was thankful for the roof over my head and set about making it my home.

I'll always remember the rush of emotions on moving day: excitement, sadness, and anxiety mingled in my heart. I felt as though I was being elevated to another stage of my life journey. My "welcome to the neighborhood" wasn't the traditional basket full of treats. Rather, it was a harsh confrontation on the second-floor landing of my new building. A man met my greeting with a spit to my face and a swift strike, knocking the box from my hands. His words were stinging: "We don't need no more fucking crackers here, go back where you came from!" I can hear most of my white family; "See, look at that, they racists and hateful too! May I respond. Who purposefully made and has treated our Black family as the monster, our enemy? And what have we done to our Black family when they moved in our communities? We burned down their homes, beat them, and used to lynch them until it was deemed illegal. He had all the right to tell me go away!

Let me share a brief history of North Lawndale. It has been mired in a turbulent past since the 1960s. After the death of Martin Luther King, riots ensued, casting a long, dark shadow over the community. It was further afflicted by housing discrimination, predatory lending, and a sequence of socio-economic crises. Many businesses and residents fled, triggering job losses and a wave of abandoned properties. Poverty seized the community, a cruel and relentless invader. However, now that white people are tired of driving from the suburbs, they have decided to reclaim North Lawndale for themselves. As I type today, re-gentrification is happening, pushing out the black families as white families move in and take over! This continued re-gentrification has been going on for over 400 years across this entire nation!

Ah, the infamous narrow, winding staircases of old Chicago apartment buildings, our two and three flats! These labyrinthine paths pose their own unique challenges when it comes to moving furniture. You can manage a queen-size bed frame, maybe a standard dresser, and with a little bit of luck and a lot of patience, perhaps even a sofa. But a double-door side-by-side refrigerator? That's a tale of epic proportions!

Enter Santos, the superhero of this story! Our paths crossed at Cook County Jail, where he had been accused of murder in 1997. Despite his conviction in 2002 and a 12-year sentence, Santos always insisted on his innocence. An FBI investigation in 2003 corroborated his claim, leading to his release on Christmas Eve that year - quite the holiday miracle!

Santos, a native of Puerto Rico, had relocated to the US with his family in a bid to secure better healthcare for his son, who was battling severe brain damage. However, his life took a dark turn when a deceitful "friend" framed him for a murder he didn't commit. Even more shocking was the apathy of his public defender, who, suspected of having ulterior motives, failed to confirm Santos's solid alibi - that he was at work, clocked in, and had numerous witnesses to back him up. As a result, Santos was declared guilty, a verdict that shattered his faith in the system.

Restoring Santos's trust in humanity became a mission for me, and it was an honor to contribute to this endeavor. Fortune eventually smiled upon Santos in 2006 when he received compensation for his wrongful conviction with the help of James D. Montgomery & Associates

formerly known as "The Cochran Firm, yes, the famous Johnny Cochran. The funds provided a lifeline, enabling Santos to secure his family's future and afford the medical care his son desperately needed.

Fast-forward to my moving day. Santos was working at Sears at the time and was able to assist me with my need for new appliances. I had bought a massive French-door refrigerator without considering the challenge of maneuvering it up my new home's narrow staircase. Santos, however, proved his mettle. In a display of sheer strength and ingenuity, he removed the refrigerator doors, strapped the behemoth to his back, and ascended the three flights of stairs with astonishing ease. Even in recollection, his feat leaves me in awe. And when it was time for the refrigerator to exit, he performed the same Herculean task in reverse!

For nearly two decades, I lived in this overlooked neighborhood, primarily home to Black families who often found themselves marginalized. It was here that I witnessed the harsh effects of white supremacy. However, it was also here that I observed a resilience that I deeply admire. These communities, despite being pushed to the brink, stood tall, reflecting Maya Angelou's iconic words, "You may shoot me with your words, You may cut me with your eyes, You may kill me with your hatefulness, But still, like air, I'll rise."

TO THE CONCRETE JUNGLE

After my spiritual awakening, like unto Nehemiah's experience with God, I dedicated my life to serving Him where ever that would be. I pledged to rebuild the walls of dignity torn down by the injustice that has positioned our Black brothers and sisters who we have placed at the tail end of society, if not beneath it.

Rewind to 1982, when I was just 10 years old. I watched the movie "Dream House", featuring John Schneider, who purchased land in New York's inner city and, despite immense hardship, made a significant impact. This deeply moved me, stirring a poignant realization - perhaps God was already grooming me for my life's journey.

Only in retrospection can we truly appreciate God's hand guiding our every step. I've come to understand these experiences taught me the depth of racism and equipped me for what lay ahead. As I venture into the specifics in the coming chapters, I urge my white family members to bear the discomfort. Please persist, so that you too might comprehend the anguish behind the words "Welcome to racism". And if you think your pain of being uncomfortable is bad, how do you think our Black family feel at the hands of our continued racism!

I cannot forget the incredible opportunity I had to meet the real-life principal from the inspiring movie "Lean on Me." This powerful film tells the true story of Dr. Frank

Napier (played by Robert Guillaume), a superintendent in New Jersey who witnesses East Side High School's descent into the lowest-ranking school in the state. With no other options left, Dr. Napier turns to maverick ex-teacher Joe Clark (portrayed by Morgan Freeman) to take on the role of principal and bring about a transformation in the struggling institution. Before Clark can tackle the academic challenges and raise the state exam scores, he must confront the school's gang and narcotics problems head-on.

When I heard the real-life principal speak, my heart was stirred, and I couldn't help but envision the incredible impact of making such a profound change in the lives of young people. Reflecting on these experiences, I now realize that God had been preparing me all along. Not only did I reside in the inner city, but for eight years, I worked for Chicago Public Schools as a Restorative Practices Coach, where I was sent to some of the most challenging schools. My mission was to work with the dedicated staff, inspire positive change within the educational system, and foster a sense of community by building relationships and promoting the value of every individual. I can personally attest that several schools began to witness significant transformations with in their students. I feel privileged to have been given numerous opportunities by God to inspire hope and make a difference in the lives of the youth and staff I encountered along the way.

When I moved to the west side, it felt like God had elevated me to a community where hopelessness reigned supreme. Let me share with you a brief history of North Lawndale.

North Lawndale, located on the West Side of Chicago, is one of the city's 77 community areas. It boasts significant landmarks such as the K-Town Historic District, the Foundation for Homan Square, and the Homan Square interrogation facility. Additionally, North Lawndale has the highest concentration of greystones in the entire city.

From 1918 to 1955, North Lawndale was primarily inhabited by Jewish immigrants of Russian and Eastern European origin. As these families prospered, they moved northward, leading to a dominant Jewish presence in the neighborhood. However, in the 1950s, a large number of black residents migrated from the South Side and southern states, seeking better opportunities. Unfortunately, unscrupulous real estate dealers used blockbusting and scare tactics to drive out the white population, resulting in a drastic decrease from 87% to less than 9%. Despite this, the total number of residents increased.

The 1960s marked a tumultuous period for North Lawndale. Riots, housing discrimination, predatory lending, and other socioeconomic disasters caused businesses and residents to leave, leaving behind a wave of job losses, abandoned properties, and widespread poverty.

In 1966, the iconic Rev. Dr. Martin Luther King Jr. visited North Lawndale and personally experienced the deplorable living conditions. Broken doors and rodent infestations were just some of the issues plaguing the community. In response, the Contract Buyers League, a grassroots organization, was established in 1968 to combat the discriminatory and predatory housing practices that targeted the area.

The loss of thousands of jobs due to industrial restructuring from the 1960s to the 1980s plunged North Lawndale into even deeper poverty. Money became scarce, leading to a lack of property maintenance. Houses were abandoned, and many structures were eventually demolished. However, in the 2000s, the neighborhood experienced a building and real estate boom, bringing renewed hope.

During my time in North Lawndale, I had the privilege of spending moments with Mr. Muldrow, the owner of Del-

Kar Drugs Inc. He shared stories about the rich history he experienced living in the community. Mr. Muldrow's pharmacy had been moved from a predominantly white community that didn't welcome black businesses.

As we flipped through his photo albums, Mr. Muldrow showed me pictures of himself with Dr. Martin Luther King Jr., highlighting the pharmacy as a place where King would buy his daily newspaper during his time in Chicago. He also shared stories about the Black Panthers, whose local headquarters was just a block away from his pharmacy. Remarkably, his pharmacy shared a building with the Conservative Vice Lords, a notorious street gang.

During the riots following King's assassination in 1968, the white-owned pharmacies in the area were ransacked. However, Mr. Muldrow shared how he was originally concerned for the safety of his pharmacy, but was reassured by the Vice Lords that they would protect it. They told him, "Go home. We're not gonna let anybody touch you."

One photo captured Mr. Muldrow with President Lyndon Johnson, where he served as a liaison between the Conservative Vice Lords Inc. The Conservative Vice Lords, in 1967, embarked on a mission to create a strong, socially conscious black community. They reached out to the youth who had begun terrorizing the community with violence and criminal activity. By providing support, tutoring, and even employment opportunities they helped turn their lives around. Initiatives like Teen Town were established, and they opened snack shops, an ice cream parlor, and even two Tasty Freeze franchises in 1968.

But what happened to these efforts? Mr. Muldrow had a story to tell. These activist-gang members built African-themed clothing stores, community currency exchanges, and civic institutions exclusively for their black compatriots. In 1969, they formed a historic alliance known as the "LSD" with the Blackstone Rangers and the Gangster Disciples, setting aside their differences to combat white supremacy. However, the city could only tolerate their defiance for so long. In 1970, despite gang-related crime being at an all-time low, Mayor Daley retaliated with a war on gangs. This led to an enormous showdown between the powers that be and the movement the Conservative Vice Lords had helped create. Some disappeared, and many were imprisoned, as the city and nation refused to let black men empower their communities.

I treasured the moments spent with Mr. Muldrow. I once asked his son if my presence was burdensome, but he assured me that his father loved sharing these stories, especially with someone like me, a white man who cared. Sadly, Mr. Muldrow has since passed away, but I hope these paragraphs bring a smile to his face, knowing that I not only cared but am committed to sharing this truth with the world.

During my first visit to Nigeria in 2002, I formed a close bond with Pastor Chris, who founded a church in Port Harcourt. The people living around his church constructed their homes using cardboard and plywood. They walked long distances, carrying water on their heads for drinking, washing, and cooking. Witnessing their living conditions broke my heart, but their resilient smiles concealed their struggles.

The following year, Pastor Chris visited me in the United States, and I took him to 16th Street to show him the property I had purchased to build Studio 29:11 and the people God had called me to serve. Within minutes, Pastor Chris pleaded with me, "Oh Pastor Dana, get me out of here! Please, I cannot bear this any longer!" Once out of the community, we pulled over, and I asked him to help me understand. I acknowledged the poverty in the area, but at least most people had homes, cable TV, and running water. I was perplexed by the dire circumstances of those he ministered to.

"Pastor Dana, those you saw may lack material possessions and running water, but they have hope," Pastor Chris explained. "They believe that tomorrow the rain they have been waiting for may come. However, here in America, my people lack hope, and without hope, you will die in darkness. That is why I had to leave. Give hope, teach hope, and watch how lives will be transformed. I couldn't do what you do, but know that God has personally chosen you, my brother."

Spreading hope came at a price. I lost most of my childhood friends, family, and the familiar aspects of my culture. But those who align themselves with the will of the Father became my new family. My identity is rooted in Christ, and my home is God's Kingdom. Over the years, I have shed countless tears, not only for my personal losses but also for the ongoing rejection of truth. This journey through the "Concrete Jungle" has exposed the pain behind those three powerful words that altered the course of my life: "Welcome to racism"!

I know you've heard countless stories about the black inner-city neighborhoods, and North Lawndale is no exception. The news often highlights the violence, drive-by shootings, gangs, and drug problems plaguing these communities. You've seen the littered streets, dilapidated buildings, overgrown vacant lots, and barred windows. Negative thoughts about these neighborhoods and the people who reside in them may have taken hold in your mind. However, before we move forward, I want to take a moment to share a few of the beautiful things you'll find in these communities. These are experiences you'll never truly understand unless you've lived there.

During the harsh Chicago winters, we mostly stayed indoors. On rare pleasant days, we would briefly chat with neighbors from our cars to our houses. After heavy snowfalls, we banded together, helping one another dig out our cars and homes. Snowblowers were a luxury we couldn't afford, so we found creative ways to clear our streets. Unfortunately, being on the west side meant our streets were never a priority. We were often shocked if they were cleaned at all, and when they were, it took days after the snowfall. In contrast, when I lived in Rogers Park, which was developing into a predominantly white community once again, even my alleys would be plowed. This is just one example of how injustice and racism have permeated every aspect of our lives.

Now, let me unveil the hidden beauty of our inner-city communities, the stories you won't hear or see in the news. Yes, it's true that we live in what may seem like a "war" zone, but adversity has only brought us residents closer together. One of the ways we fostered unity and created a sense of family was through our Block Club, led by the incredible Ms. Carol. She was unwavering in her commitment to keeping our block beautiful and ensuring the children felt loved.

The Block Club had dedicated leaders who regularly met to address any issues that arose. They upheld the standards we set for living on the 1200 Spaulding block. A sign greeted all visitors turning down our street, a reminder of our shared responsibilities: "Please drive slow, we have children here; please lower music after 9pm; Please respect each other, we are in this together." Thanks to the efforts of our Block Club, our block shone like a diamond in the rough. We took immense pride in our well-maintained lawns, and we supported one another in keeping them looking as good as possible.

Watching after the children was one of the Block Club's primary responsibilities. Every summer, we obtained a city permit to block off the street for a day of festivities, especially for the kids. We rented bouncing houses, arranged pony rides, and set up a dunk tank, among other exciting activities. The adults brought out their grills to the front yard, and I must admit that Anthony and his boys were much better grillers than I ever was. Andre, until his sudden passing, brought out his speakers and served as our DJ. The entire block resonated with the sounds of laughter, music, and the joyful cries of kids. We became a family bound by love rather than blood.

As night fell, the music transitioned into slow jams. The adults gathered for card games and table games, while others took to dancing in the streets. The rest of us found solace on various porches, engaging in conversations and relishing the escape from the realities of life. On those special summer days, we shattered our self-imposed 9pm quiet time, dancing into the night. No one complained, not even our seniors, who joined in the festivities, showcasing their dance moves on that very street. I cherished these moments, as well as the Sunday nights when a neighbor would open his garage door in the early evening and play slow jams until late at night. I sat on my porch, marveling at my black family and their incredible resilience, strength, and ability to infuse joy and happiness into any environment. I felt deeply honored that my white skin was never merely tolerated but always loved and embraced. I never had to endure a burning cross in my front yard or a swastika spray-painted on my home. They saw beyond the color of my skin just as Martin Luther King quoted; "I have a dream that my four little children will one day live in a nation where they will not be judged by the color of their skin but by the content of their character."

I will say that on this one Saturday night, while I was upstairs speaking to my parents, I thought rocks were being thrown at my house. My mind immediately jumped to the incident earlier that day when my Rottweiler, Deborah, had gotten loose and approached some kids playing on the 1300 block of Spaulding. They didn't know that she only wanted to play, but I also would have ran! I did get her to come back before she reached them. But in a moment of panic from the noise, I rushed downstairs to see what was happening, only to discover that we were being bombarded by a hailstorm with hail the size of golf balls and even larger! By the time the storm subsided, most of our cars were completely smashed, and some windows in our homes were shattered. I endured over 50,000 of damage! But the bigger issues was my heart. I was ashamed of myself for briefly entertaining the thought that those moms would retaliate by stoning my home, a remnant of the racist mindset I needed to let go. Ten months later, while in St. Louis, I encountered another storm that totaled my car. State Farm canceled my insurance after that incident.

Our Block Club also made sure that every school-aged child had the necessary supplies when they returned to school in the fall. Every student received a backpack filled with essential items, ensuring that no child would fail due to a lack of resources. We also distributed coats and other necessities to those in need. The Reynolds, a kind-hearted family, opened their home who lived at the end of the block to tutor hundreds of kids over the years. As I said, we were family.

I was grateful for the Candy Lady, who had an assortment of small candies and treats to include snow cones and Honey Buns, all at a lower cost than the stores. And almost every day, the ice cream truck would grace our block with its presence, causing all of us to excitedly rush out and enjoy a delicious, refreshing treat even though the "Ice Cream Truck Song" got on my very last nerve.

See it's a widely shared experience to chase after the ice cream truck upon hearing its jingle, but few are aware of its racist origins in the minstrel shows of the early 1900s. The song originally began as "Turkey in the Straw," but in 1916, vaudeville actor Harry C. Browne changed the lyrics to "N***** Love A Watermelon, Ha! Ha! Ha!" It's important to acknowledge and confront the problematic history attached to such cultural phenomena.

During those scorching summer days, you could always find relief by joining us in running through the refreshing spray of our fire hydrant water sprinkler! We would remove the cap and then carefully position a car tire around the hydrant to hold a 2x4 in front of the spout. The tire acted as a stabilizer, allowing the water to shoot into the air, reaching heights of 10 feet or more. The force of this powerful sprinkler not only brought relief from the heat but also served as a convenient way to give your car a thorough wash.

As I mentioned before, we became a family. This didn't mean we were free from disagreements, just like any family. But when it came down to it, no disagreement was more significant than our love and respect for one another. Ms. Carol and Mrs. Kitty, always vigilant, kept their eyes open for anything out of the ordinary. They swiftly made calls to ensure everyone's safety and well-being if something should arise. Whenever I left for an extended period, a simple notification to these ladies was all I needed, and everything would be taken care of.

For over 15 years, I was neighbors with the Ollies, who had four sons. I initially got to know Troy, the second youngest, who joined me in my ministry outreach on 16th street. Over the years, however, all the Ollie boys became like family to me including their precious Mom Mrs. Gail. Many days, Mr. Ollie and I would sit on the porch and engage in heartfelt conversations. Our homes were merely eight feet apart. During our time together, Mr. Ollie opened his heart, sharing his past mistakes and the periods of depression that seemed to resurface, preventing him from moving forward. He became a symbol of how this unjust system holds our black men back that even years later his past dealings with the law kept him from securing a job, and I am talking about years and years later! To see this downward cycle in Mr. Ollie's loosing hope truly affected me as well.

I will forever carry the weight of the conversation I had with Mr. Ollie, etched deeply in my heart. It was a solemn moment, as we sat on our back decks, exchanging raw emotions. His words pierced through the air, laden with a mix of disappointment and resignation. "Well, Dana, I have to confess that when we first moved in and saw we would be living next to a white man, I couldn't help but think, 'Damn, can we ever catch a break?' Even in this community, I have to be neighbors with a white man. But I must say, over the years, my feelings have transformed into love and respect for you. I am grateful that you have been my neighbor." His voice trembled with sincerity as he continued, "Now, I need you to make me a promise. Promise me that you will always look after my boys. I know you're a good man, and I want you to promise me this." I felt a mixture of confusion and admiration for Mr. Ollie's heartfelt plea. "Mr. Ollie, despite the hardships you've faced, you've been an incredible father. Your boys have you." But he insisted, his eyes pleading, "Please, promise me, Dana." And so, with a heavy heart, I made that promise.

Tragically, just three days later, I received the devastating news that Mr. Ollie had passed away from a massive stroke. The weight of his absence settled upon our community, leaving a void that could never be filled. At his funeral, I shared the story of our conversation, the depth of his love for his family, and the immense responsibility I now carried. I vowed to do everything in my power to honor my promise to Mr. Ollie. However, life's harsh realities took their toll, and we experienced yet another heart-wrenching loss. Marcel, the eldest son, succumbed to medical complications. The pain of these losses shook our neighborhood, yet Byron, Troy, Nathan, and Ms. Gale remained resilient, doing their best to navigate life's challenges. Their strength in the face of adversity continues to inspire me.

To my left, there was Ben, my neighbor and a lifelong resident of our community. His weathered two-flat building stood as a testament to the passage of time, its second floor displaying visible signs of decay. Despite his age, Ben continued to toil tirelessly, well beyond what retirement should have allowed. Almost every day, he would push his trusty shopping cart around the block, scouring for discarded cans and scrap metal to turn into meager cash. "Extra cash is always handy these days," he would say with a hint of resignation. Whenever I faced issues with my home or lawnmower, it was Ben who would find a way to fix them.

Mr. Ben was a man of faith, an elder at his church, whose devotion to loving God and loving people radiated from his very being. I witnessed the struggles he faced in simply navigating through life. His car would break down, and he would painstakingly save up every penny to purchase the necessary parts. Yet, I never heard a word of complaint escape his lips. Instead, he would search for solutions with unwavering determination. But one day, he came over and sat at my dining room table, the weight of the world etched upon his face. The city of Chicago had issued him a warning, demanding that his aging back porches and outdoor stairs be replaced with metal ones. There had been a few incidents of porches collapsing, causing injuries, so the city was cracking down on these safety violations. Unfortunately, Ben's property was one of the first to be cited.

With tears streaming down his weathered cheeks, I will forever carry the weight of his words and the profound pain of his struggle. "I just can't do this anymore, Dana. I'm tired. I don't have $25,000 to replace my back steps, and if I can't, they'll condemn my property. I'm tired." Ben was not only a devoted citizen but also an American veteran, yet the government seemed indifferent to his plight. The next chapter of Ben's story unfolded tragically as he was diagnosed with cancer, his weary body succumbing to the relentless battle within. With a heavy heart, I bid farewell to this remarkable man as I know. Yes, we say it was cancer, but I know differently, it was exhaustion and deep hopelessness. But now his precious soul has finally been released to find solace in an eternal paradise.

These are just a few glimpses into the rich tapestry of life within our inner-city communities. This chapter by no means can contain all the beauty I have stored in my heart from my years of being blessed to live amongst my black family. So know, behind the negative stereotypes, the struggles, and the hardships, lies a vibrant and resilient community that exemplifies the true meaning of family and perseverance. To all my family back on the 1200 block of Spaulding, thank you and I love you all!

Tupac Shakur said it best, "Long live the rose that grew from concrete when no one else even cared. Only God can judge me. You never know how strong you can be until being strong is the only choice you have left."

THE MOUTH OF THE SERPENT

In 2002, I joined The Navigators, a global Christian organization based in Colorado Springs, Colorado. Its mission revolves around mentoring Christians, honing their spiritual growth, and enabling them to spread their faith. Essentially, it's a haven for those who are mission-minded, offering accountability, spiritual nourishment, and support. We served as missionaries, fueling our mission through sponsorships from individuals, churches, and organizations. Though we had missionaries stationed worldwide, I served right here in Chicago as an Urban Missionary.

During a trip to raise support, a young lady approached me after my talk. "Dana," she said, "are you receptive to visions? If so, I've received one for you. May I share it?" Intrigued and a believer in the mystical myself, I gave my consent.

She painted a vivid image of God lowering me into the gaping maw of a monstrous serpent. In her vision, I clung to God with one arm, while using the other to pull both young and old black men from the beast's jaws. She saw me wounded, scratched, bruised and at times bleeding profusely by the serpent's teeth, but the divine promise was that the serpent would never swallow me, he would never be able to close his mouth on me. I was destined to venture where few would dare, snatching these men from the brink, enduring great suffering, but never being destroyed, crushed, or forsaken.

Over the years, God has communicated through dreams and visions, reinforcing that this path He set me on wouldn't be easy; it would be filled with pain. But His promise echoed the words of Joshua 1:9, reinforcing strength, courage, and unwavering divine support.

Upon my return home on the west side, I resumed my prayer walks I started along 16th Street, much like I used to do on Morse Avenue when I lived in Rogers Park on the north side. This street was notorious known as a drug-infested, with rampant gang activity, and lots of chilling despair. It was Morse Avenue on steroids, but my calling was now here, so I walked and prayed with unwavering boldness and conviction just as I did up north.

One day, as I strolled past a group of young black men, I overheard them questioning my regular presence, suspecting me of being an undercover 5-0 (cop). Sensing their pursuit, I quickened my pace without breaking stride, continuing my prayers, seeking divine protection.

Suddenly, an older black man joined me. After a few steps, he said, "Young man, you're called by God to be here, to touch many lives. If God weren't with you, you'd be dead by now. You're walking in the mouth of the serpent!" Instantly, I remembered the vision and those prophetic words.

He told me of a time when this street was a vibrant hub before the Martin Luther King Jr. riots. He pointed at a crumbling building, recalling how MLK himself once frequented it. But now, the street was known as the blood path because of the bloodshed and death. He recounted a horrifying tale of a woman being decapitated and her head paraded around down 16th street from Pulaski to Central. "The Blood Path. The mouth of the serpent!" he said. "Thank you, young man, for bringing a light of hope into this darkness." He left, disappearing into the urban maze, never to be seen again.

MY NEED FOR A COKE!

My frequent strolls down 16th Street I pray would be a testament to my unwavering faith and resilience. Not all of my stories from those walks ended the same way, but one thing was consistent — they all reinforced the beautiful fact that serving God was the best decision I'd ever made.

One such afternoon, as I paced the streets with prayers on my lips, a group of about five guys began to trail me. They hurled abuses and assorted small objects at me, including glass bottles. One hit me in the back and another found my head. Thankfully, they eventually diverted down a side street. I quickened my pace to my car, tending to my bleeding head with an aspirin and a napkin before heading straight home.

That very night, around 10:30, a sudden craving for a soda and snack seized me. Most stores were closed by then due to the neighborhood's reputation, but I recalled a gas station a few blocks away on Roosevelt Road. Much like how we order groceries online today, the attendant would fetch items for late-night customers while we waited outside at the revolving bullet proof window. I acquired my soda and Snickers bar and was heading back to my car when a man approached me.

"Excuse me, sir, can I get some change?" The man's request caught me off guard. I responded honestly, "Sorry, man, I don't have anything on me. I used my card." But my answer didn't satisfy him. With each repeated plea, his frustration grew. "No, man, you just don't understand, do you? I need some money!" I reiterated, "I'm sorry, man, I don't have any."

To my surprise, four other men appeared, surrounding my car. They blocked my path, attempting to prevent me from entering. With quick thinking and a narrow opening, I managed to unlock and maneuver myself through. I squeezed my body, thanking God for my slender frame at the time. Some of the men positioned themselves behind me, but I pleaded with them, rolling down my window. I urged them to move, fearing someone might get hurt. "Guys, please, God knows I don't have anything for you. I just want to go home without causing harm. Let's avoid violence, and let God be my witness to my innocence." Slowly, I put my car in reverse, relieved as they finally stepped aside. The sound of a beer bottle hitting my back window echoed in my ears, but I was grateful it didn't shatter.

It was only when I reached the safety of my home that the full weight of what had just transpired hit me. My mind, body, and spirit finally connected, and the reality of the situation washed over me. I am far from superhuman, but God has granted me strength and peace during moments like these. I took a moment to relish in the victory over my carnal desires, knowing that divine protection had guided me through this harrowing encounter.

The next evening, around the same time, I found myself craving a soda again. I hesitated, given the previous night's events, but then I recalled my father's wisdom when I fell off my bike as a child. He encouraged me to get back on to conquer my fear. Spurred by this memory, I decided to confront my fear and headed back to the gas station.

Successfully procuring my soda, I returned to my car, whispering a thankful prayer.

I sat in my car, relieved and grateful. As I took a moment to breathe and thank God, a knock on my window startled me. It was a Black man standing outside. I felt a twinge of apprehension, knowing that I couldn't allow the actions of others who shared his skin color to define him. I had made a choice to fight against this and to understand the pain experienced by those first five young men, even when that pain was directed at me.

With a mixture of curiosity and caution, I rolled down the window and greeted him, "Hey, man." His voice trembled with sincerity as he spoke, "Sir, sir, aren't you that white guy who was walking on 16th street a day or so ago?" I confirmed that it was indeed me. What he said next shook me to my core.

"I found out that you're a good guy, and I want to ask for your forgiveness," he pleaded. "The other day, I was with those guys who were calling you names. It was my bottle that hit you in the back of the head. I had to come and apologize to you. I'm really sorry."

Tears streamed down my face as I opened the car door and embraced him. In that moment, I couldn't hold back my overwhelming emotions. "Young man," I said through my tears, "not only do I forgive you, but I have immense respect for a man who has the courage to apologize." In that powerful encounter, the barriers of resentment and division crumbled, replaced by understanding, empathy, and the transformative power of forgiveness.

This young man, Marcus, shared his struggles, mirroring those of many others in the neighborhood, who lost hope and turned to drugs. God led me to connect Marcus with a trade school and a GED program. About a year later, I heard a familiar voice calling me — it was Marcus. He had successfully completed his GED, graduated from trade school, and was on the path to bettering his life. We shared a hug, and I expressed how proud I was of him and how much he inspired me.

That was the last I saw of Marcus, but his impact on my life was profound. He not only helped me confront my fears but also understand God's voice more distinctly. His courage and redemption served as a living testimony of hope and transformation. I thank Marcus, and more importantly, I thank God for these experiences — for they truly shape us and bring us closer to understanding His divine purpose.

OH ISAIAH!

Throughout my tenure at Cook County Jail, I encountered countless amazing individuals, each with their unique talents, capabilities, and creativity. I was astounded by their ingenious methods of survival. They demonstrated resourcefulness, transforming mundane objects like milk cartons to heat makeshift griddles to prepare meals with ingredients from the commissary. Crafted items from recycled wrappers further accentuated their inventive spirits. I have several drawings hanging on my walls that bring so many memories, both sad and happy. Sad to know where these men will spend the majority of their life, but happy I had the privilege of sharing some of our life together. However, their potential trapped within the prison walls stirred a deep ache within me. How tragically we, as a society, had failed these men!

Among these men, a few managed to wrangle freedom. Their charges were reduced or dismissed entirely. One such individual was Isaiah. A young man of 24 when I met him, he was released at 27 after serving his time. I still remember the early morning call from him. "Hey Pastor, they released me, but when I reached my Mom's house, she was gone. I have no idea where she might be. I spent the entire night on the train, nowhere to go. Could you help me out?"

At the time, I was working with ministry partners to acquire a building for a transitional home for individuals leaving correctional centers. But why wait? I had a three-bedroom apartment with two vacant rooms that Fletch was allowing me to live for free, how selfish I would be to not share in this blessing, especially when an emergency. So, Isaiah moved in, and together we established guidelines and goals for his transition to independence.

For the first month, Isaiah was diligent, attending his GED classes and actively job-hunting. However, by the second month, his motivation waned. He stopped going to class, halted his job search, and spent most of his time watching TV. I had a sinking feeling that he was drifting into illicit activities.

One particular afternoon, Isaiah departed early. I had been cleaning, taking out the trash when I suddenly experienced a bizarre sensation — it felt as though my head was detaching from my body. I had never felt anything like this before. Was I dying? Was I losing my sanity? Or perhaps, I was just in dire need of food and water? Unable to stand any longer, I lay down on my bed and, a few hours later, woke up feeling normal again. What had happened remained a mystery.

Not long after waking up, Fletch, the owner of the building, dropped by for a casual visit. We walked into the kitchen to grab bottled water, but Fletch abruptly halted after a few steps into the kitchen. "My God, where is it?" he blurted out. Confused, I asked, "Where is what, Fletch?" His answer left me stunned, "The cocaine, my body is reacting to it!"

I looked up to see this towering 6'4" man standing rigid, beads of sweat trickling down his face as he started to shake. It was then I relayed to him the strange incident I had experienced earlier. "You had a contact high, what did you touch?" he questioned. Tracing back my steps, I realized I had last touched the back doorknob while taking out the trash. That's where the residue was.

"Dana, Isaiah can't stay here any longer, this is serious!" Fletch stated with alarming certainty. Was I mad, sad, hurt, furious, or a mix of all these emotions? I couldn't exactly tell, but one thing was clear: I had recognized the signs and knew that I was ill-equipped to help Isaiah in this struggle. Resolute, I decided, "Tomorrow, after church, I will sit down with Isaiah and arrange for his relocation come Monday."

Isaiah arrived home late that night and missed church the following morning. I left a note for him, expressing my wish to talk once I returned. As I pulled up to my apartment building after church, there stood Isaiah, a frantic look on his face. He sprinted over to the car, breathlessly announcing, "Pastor, we've been robbed, and I think they've poisoned Deborah, my two-year-old Rottweiler."

My heart dropped at his words. Rushing inside, I found Deborah lifeless in the bathroom. My electronics, computer, jewelry, and other items of value were missing, but the loss of my faithful companion stung the most. Her death was a cruel reminder of losing Umoja back in Rogers Park.

Retreating to my room, I allowed my tears to fall freely, struggling to understand the series of events. How had these criminals managed to lure my 95lb German Rottweiler into the bathroom, only to poison her? Why was it only my belongings that had been stolen, and nothing from Isaiah's room?

Rarely did I ask God for specific guidance or signs, preferring to find comfort in the randomness of scripture. But that day, desperate for answers, I opened the Bible and found myself staring at Habakkuk 2:6 — "Woe to him who piles up stolen goods and makes himself wealthy by extortion! How long must this go on?"

The verse resonated deeply, and I felt a profound message in my heart. "Son, how long will you allow this to continue in your home?" It was God answering my plea, affirming my suspicions, and nudging me to make a decisive choice about my living situation with Isaiah.

As upset as I was, my heart felt heavy with sorrow, accepting the hard truth — Isaiah was the orchestrator of this debacle. Yet, when confronted, Isaiah denied any involvement in the robbery. "I loved Deborah, why would I do anything to hurt her?" he argued. However, when I brought up the cocaine residue, he fell silent, stood up, and began to pack his belongings. "Do you want your computer back?" he asked me, to which I replied, "No, Isaiah, whatever I gave you is still yours." Isaiah remained quiet and invisible until the following afternoon when he emerged from his room, carrying boxes filled with his possessions.

Our journey ended on the south side. With heartfelt goodbyes exchanged, I offered Isaiah a prayer and a comforting hug. "Please, Isaiah, you're a good man, don't let your life end like this," I implored. Silence was his only reply as he watched me climb into my car and drive away, possibly for the last time.

Fast-forward two years, an unexpected call jolted me. "Is this Pastor Stevens?" asked a voice. "I'm a nurse caring for a young man named Isaiah, who has requested me to contact you. Isaiah was shot several times a few months back, and we're hoping to discharge him in the upcoming weeks. He wishes to see you before he leaves."

Walking into his hospital room, I struggled to keep my emotions in check. Isaiah was a shadow of his former self. A bullet had shattered his left hip, another had ripped through his right elbow, leaving his arm limp and useless, and yet another lodged in his upper thigh. Walking with a cane, he seemed to have aged decades overnight. I rushed to his side, wrapping him in a tight embrace. "Oh Isaiah," I whispered.

Tears welled up in his eyes. "I'm so sorry, Pastor, for all the pain I've caused you. Can you ever forgive me?" he pleaded. Our second hug was warmer, more assuring, as I answered, "Yes Isaiah, I forgive you."

Our conversation flowed smoothly, unveiling his living conditions before the shooting — in his car, riddled with over a dozen bullets, five of which found him. His survival was deemed a miracle by the doctors. "See Isaiah, I always knew you were a fighter. Don't give up now," I encouraged him, wrapping him in a final goodbye hug. Isaiah reached out occasionally over the following months, but then, the calls ceased.

Two years later, another phone call shattered the silence. "Is this Pastor Stevens? We're calling from the Cook County Coroner's office. We're trying to locate a relative who could claim the body of a certain Isaiah. His emergency contact information at the hospital only listed you. Can you help us get in touch with any family member, his mom or dad perhaps?" I could only reply with a heavy 'no'. "If you happen to find any information, please let us know. His body will remain here until then," they concluded. As I hung up the phone, tears streaked down my face. "Oh Isaiah," I murmured.

LET'S PLAY FAMILY FEUD!

Growing up, I was enamored with game shows. I still chuckle when I recall my younger self, pencil in hand, eagerly jotting down bids while watching The Price is Right, rooting for contestants on Wheel of Fortune, Press Your Luck, and Card Sharks. The thrill of seeing people win, especially when it was something they genuinely needed like a car, was infectious.

One of my favorites was Family Feud. At times, certain families would struggle to score any points, and I'd find myself questioning why some of the members were included in the team. They might have been better off recruiting a knowledgeable neighbor!

So, why dedicate an entire chapter to Family Feud, you might wonder? Well, one particular episode of this show offered a profound insight.

In this episode, a white family was pitted against a black family. The black family was remarkably quick with the buzzer, winning control of the game each time. The show's structure relied on responses from surveys conducted across America, effectively capturing the popular opinion.

The final question was the game-changer. The black family, ahead by a significant margin, had to answer: "Name something you eat for Thanksgiving Day meal." As usual, they were the first to hit the buzzer and promptly responded with "Turkey!", the top answer. Opting to play, they moved on to the next family member. "Mac and Cheese!", they exclaimed, only to be met with a red 'X' on the screen, indicating an incorrect answer. The same fate awaited the answer "Sweet potato pie!"

Steve Harvey, the show's host, re-read the question and issued a warning. They already had two strikes. One more incorrect answer and the other family would have a chance to steal. If they succeeded, they would win the round, and with it, the game, thanks to the tripled points in the final round. Unfazed, the next family member confidently replied, "Spaghetti!" But alas, a third red 'X' appeared.

Now, the white family had a chance to not only win the round but also the entire game. They deliberated and settled on the answer "ham," which ultimately clinched their victory. As the unrevealed answers surfaced, I felt an epiphany wash over me — a realization that this game show was more than just entertainment. It carried a potent message, one worth sharing in my book.

The black family didn't lose because they were less intelligent or capable. They lost because the society they lived in was designed to favor the white family's experiences and traditions. In essence, to secure victory, the black family would have had to provide answers in line with a traditional white family's Thanksgiving Dinner. They were at a disadvantage from the get-go.

As the years went by, I recognized this biased structure in the tests and exams students had to navigate throughout their academic journey. These assessments often reflected white society, culture, traditions, and norms, thereby undermining the performance of black students and reinforcing societal inequalities.

The ACT and college entrance exams also displayed similar biases, unjustly setting black students up for failure or limiting their access to certain colleges and universities. I witnessed this inequality persisting in everyday curriculum and unit tests, systematically placing black students at a disadvantage compared to their white peers, from school to college and beyond, into society as a whole.

Throughout the years, I've come to a sobering realization about the workings of white supremacy. It exercises its might by strategically propagating what serves its interests and persistently fuels stereotypes that cast the black man as a wild horse - an idea vividly depicted in the book "The Willie Lynch Letters". These structures appear to flourish under such conditions. Yet, it's crucial to comprehend that the perceived "triumph" is achieved solely through disadvantaging the black man, systematically undermining him to retain dominance. Buried deep within, we, as white people, inherently acknowledge the extraordinary strength of the black man, whether we voice this recognition or not. White America is afraid of the black man and the only way we can keep him down is by making his life a struggle on every turn. This is a truth we must face and a dialogue we must courageously embrace.

HE'S REACHING

Growing up, I saw cops as allies! My only concern was to follow the laws! If I did that, I was safe because cops were there to protect and help us! This notion began in grade school when a local officer would come to share safety tips and assure us that the police were there to assist us whenever we needed, they were our friends!

However, this perception drastically shifted when I moved into a predominantly black inner-city neighborhood. I learned that police officers were not always the friends I once believed them to be; in fact, some seemed more like foes. My resentment towards them began to swell as I started witnessing the numerous injustices occurring around me. While social media does play a part in revealing the injustices faced by our black brethren, living in a black community provides a complete perspective. And trust me, the transgressions highlighted on social media barely scratch the surface of the countless injustices taking place.

While I was in Rogers Park at the Church, eager young people wanting to be the first on the basketball court would often gather by the door about 15 minutes before I arrived. Between my full-time job and volunteering at Cook County Jail and the Juvenile Detention Center, I was often rushing to make it on time. My basketball outreach initiative became renowned throughout the community and even attracted city-wide attention. I was honored with the "Spirit of Rogers Park" award for Youth Leadership from the City of Chicago and, a few years later, received the "Guardian of the Future" award from Inspired Partnerships and the Richard H Driehaus Foundation!

One particular day, the usual crowd of eager youngsters was conspicuously absent, and no one showed up at all. I sensed that something was amiss. As I was about to leave the church, one of our "shorties," as we affectionately call our young people, walked in, tears streaming down his face, holding his dirty and trampled baseball cap in his hands. "We were just waiting to play basketball when the cops showed up and told us to go home," he sobbed. "One of them knocked off my cap, threw it on the ground, and stomped on it. Now my Christmas present from my Dad is ruined!" I attempted to file a complaint at the station, but the officer at the desk implicitly discouraged me, suggesting it would be ill-advised to do so.

In the preceding chapters, I've shared various accounts of the challenges that I faced during my initial eight years living in the inner-city. These incidents served as tests from the Lord to humble me, to shape my heart, and to foster empathy. My car was broken into over 10 times during that period, and my home suffered three break-ins, including one terrifying burglary during which I found myself hiding under my basement stairs, praying that the intruders would not discover me, while I listened to the sounds of my home being ransacked.

After one of the break-ins, I called the police, but they never arrived, so I had to visit the police station myself to file a report for my insurance. Another time, it took multiple calls and six hours before they finally showed up. As they entered through my kicked-in door, their initial words stung: "You should have told us you were white; we would've been here hours ago! Remember that for next time." I spent the remainder of their visit defending my choice to live in a neighborhood that they referred to with a derogatory term I refuse to repeat. Therefore, when the burglary occurred, I decided not to call the police. I silently waited for the thieves to leave, snapped some pictures for evidence, and drove to the station myself to file the break-in report for my insurance. After that incident, I never again called upon the police for help.

I can't count how many times I've been pulled over with officers justifying their actions by stating, "We thought you were here to buy drugs." Once, in response to this assumption, I retorted, "Officer, if I fit the stereotype of a drug buyer, then why aren't there more white guys at Cook County Jail? I see all the black drug dealers there." Over time, my patience wore thin, and I found myself frequently in confrontations - handcuffed, pushed onto the hood of my car, with my groceries dumped on the ground, revealing my prescription medications. "Look, he's a sick one," an officer once mockingly jeered.

One incident, however, is indelibly etched in my memory. I was pulled over just across the street from my house, on my way home from the gym. While at the gym my rear license plate had fallen off, which I'd placed on the car floor with the intention to fix once I got home. As I saw the flashing lights in my rearview mirror, I rolled down my window. The officers began questioning me, "May we see your driver's license? What are you doing on this side of the city? Got anything in the car we should know about? Your back license plate is missing." I explained, "Yes, it fell off at the gym. It's on the floor behind me. I can show you." As I instinctively reached behind to grab the license plate, the officer yelled, "He's reaching behind his seat!" A chilling wave of realization washed over me – had I been black, this would have been the end of my life.

That incident led me to countless hours of reflection, thinking about the innocent black men who lost their lives because they reacted naturally, just as I had done, in trying to show proof to the officers. That day, my skin color saved my life. But my heart aches for my black brothers and sisters whose skin color became a tragic liability. This chapter is dedicated to all of them, with the hope that my story will help amplify theirs, shedding light on the stark realities of racial inequities in our society.

LOST IN THE JUNGLE!

During the summer of 2004 while with the Navigators, I was entrusted with leading a dynamic team of college students to Bandung, Indonesia. Set against a backdrop of stunning volcanoes and idyllic tea plantations, Bandung, the capital of West Java province, was a city brimming with vibrant life. Our mission? To establish a summer English program for nearly 20 high school students. The Navigators' headquarters became our communal living space, and our days were crammed with stimulating English lessons, enlightening Bible studies, and a myriad of fun activities.

We often embarked on excursions to nearby villages, nestled amid verdant rice paddies. We came bearing gifts of games, music, Bible studies, and a taste of American treats for the local children. The ten-week journey turned out to be a life-changing experience. To this day, I remain connected with several of my Indonesian brethren!

A key figure on this journey was Puji, our indispensable liaison, interpreter, and staff member from the Indonesian Navigators. Without her, our endeavor would have floundered. Post the summer camp, we set off for the Indonesian National Navigator's Conference. A 300-mile bus journey awaited us, which, to my astonishment, took nearly 22 hours! Only the combined force of my best friend Dramamine and Puji got me through as we made our way threw the wandering and curving narrow roads.

With the conference concluded, it was time to bid farewell to the American college students. They were headed back stateside, leaving Puji and me to brave an overcrowded bus ride back. The journey, which involved sitting on the floor, lasted a grueling 26 hours. But eventually, we made it back to headquarters. My last few days in Bandung were spent leisurely, soaking in the city's atmosphere before my departure.

Next, I flew to Batam, Indonesia, from Jakarta. Upon disembarking the plane, I found myself waiting for a missionary whom I had only corresponded with over email. We didn't even know what each other looked like! Amid the chaos of this potential disaster, we managed to find each other, thanks to my conspicuous presence as a white American.

We walked over to a large canoe-like wooden boat docked nearby. After stowing my bag, I took a seat in the middle, a silent observer to the unintelligible exchange between the missionary and the boatmen. With a hearty "Have a good trip," the missionary left me in their care.

That boat ride was a breathtaking experience I'll remember for a lifetime! For nearly two captivating hours, we sailed through an ever-changing tapestry of landscapes, each more awe-inspiring than the last. Islands dotted the horizon, emerging and disappearing like mirages in the vast ocean expanse.

We passed stilted villages perched delicately above the ocean, their humble dwellings hinting at a lifestyle untouched by modern amenities, with the exception of one particular village. Out of the seemingly nothingness, a colossal grey tower appeared, rising three to four stories high, its surface riddled with thousands of small brick-sized holes. To my astonishment, it was a bustling avian metropolis, with thousands of birds, Barn swallow flitting in and out of the apertures.

This village was a stark contrast to the others - it hummed with the presence of electricity. I later discovered that the villagers had harnessed the economic potential of their avian neighbors. The Chinese prized the hardened and dried bird saliva, known as yan wo, as an extravagant delicacy often used in congee, soup, or even savored as a dessert. The sale of this precious ingredient ensured the village's financial stability, providing them with the means to power their homes. This revelation was a testament to the resilience and resourcefulness of humanity, a spectacle that left me utterly speechless.

Sometimes our journey would hug the edge of an island with the infinite expanse of the ocean on our left, and at other times, it felt like traversing a wide river with islands flanking both sides. When we finally reached our destination, a resort in its early stages, I breathed a sigh of relief. I was to spend the next two weeks in a unique setting of huts built on stilts, connected by wooden walkways and overlooking the shore. The reason for this elevated construction became apparent as protection against land animals and a way to catch the cool ocean breezes in the face of 120-degree temperatures. I had to admit, this was an adventure unlike any I had ever experienced before, and it really hadn't even started yet.

This burgeoning resort, teetering on the edge of existence, was being constructed by an eclectic mix of volunteers, flying in from stateside. College students and other adults were lending their hands and hearts, building this paradise while exploring nearby islands and villages on evangelical missions. My purpose was to assess if we too could enter into a partnership and send student groups here in the summers to come.

A spirited group from Colorado, if my memory serves me right, was already there serving and I eagerly joined them on their daily ventures and island escapades. We'd pack into a wooden boat, designed just for our dozen. Dawn and dusk here were sharply punctuated at 5 am and 5 pm, and we were sternly warned against lingering in the jungle after dark. An advisory I needed no convincing to heed - my eyes could only penetrate the jungle's depths so far and that was already far enough for me!

The journey was serene until we entered a strait so tight that I feared our boat might scrape against the banks. As the tide receded, an intricate web of tree roots was exposed, three to four feet below the normal sea level. They loomed like bars of a prison cell, hiding curious creatures whose eyes twinkled from the depths. My central seat felt like a sanctuary, I was certain that if a jungle beast lunged at our boat, it would encounter others first.

When the river narrowed further, our motor was deemed useless and we relied on our oars to navigate the winding river route. Despite my mounting anxiety, I found myself marveling at the untamed beauty, grateful to God for this extraordinary opportunity. That is until our boat hit a snag - a low river bed that our rowing could not conquer. Our missionary guide, ever-confident, assured us men that we would simply disembark and haul the boat forward. As Whitney Houston once proclaimed, "Hell to the no!" I was far from ready to wade in murky waters, sharing space with the unknown creatures lurking beneath.

Yet, reluctantly, with heavy trepidation, I stepped into the water to fulfill my duty. One moment, the muck was knee-deep, the next, water lapped at my neck. The unpredictable terrain kept us on our toes, literally. At one point, my Croc was swallowed by the muck and I had to plunge my head underwater to retrieve it. A harrowing experience, but I emerged victorious, shoe in hand.

After a grueling 45-minute struggle, we finally reached our land destination. An hour-long hike lay ahead, leading us to a paradisiacal freshwater waterfall and spring, teeming with body-nourishing minerals. As we trudged through the terrain, we learned to wield our machetes, our constant companions on the journey. I cracked open a towering termite mound and tasted the wood-like flavor of its inhabitants. We discovered how to tap into vines for a gulp of fresh water, and used our machetes to catch crawfish, our guide enlightening us with survival skills for the unlikely event of us getting lost. My response was simple: I was sticking to our guide like glue. There was no way I was getting lost in this vast, uncharted jungle!

Our destination, a crystal-clear spring, was a solid two-hour trek away, but its invitation to swim was irresistible. The clear water promised no hidden threats, so I readily dove in, the coolness a welcome contrast to the balmy air. After an hour, however, we had to retreat, lest the dusk catch us off-guard in the jungle. The tide would be our ally, enabling us to motor our way back, saving us from the earlier exertion.

A proposal by six of the students sparked an unexpected detour. They sought permission to jog back to the boat waiting at the shoreline. One of them claimed familiarity with the trail, and their request was granted. Seeing an opportunity to flaunt my fitness regimen, I decided to join them. "See you slowpokes at the river's bank," I exclaimed, not knowing how prophetic those words would be.

The bad idea became apparent shortly into the run. Our interpretations of "jog" were evidently miles apart. Their pace quickly outstripped mine, and soon my calls fell on deaf ears. Comforting myself with the prospect of the walkers catching up, I slowed to a walk, nursing several blisters from the unforgiving Crocs and the harsh terrain. However, an unseen divergence in the path had led me astray, and unbeknownst to me, I had veered off course.

The realization dawned - I was lost in the jungle. To compound the situation, the sun was threatening to dip below the horizon, and my earlier inattentiveness to survival lessons was about to bite me. The first hour of isolation was surprisingly calm, until a lizard, resembling a Komodo dragon, crossed my path. My cry wasn't a desperate plea to God like Peter in the Bible when he yelled "Jesus"! But rather, "Oh shit", which, strangely enough, seemed to scare off the beast. My calmness, however, deserted me along with the lizard.

A fleeting moment of despair washed over me. Was this the end? From surviving the threats of Chicago to perish in the jungle? I sank to my knees, tears of desperation staining the jungle floor, as the gloom of the setting sun deepened. A heartfelt plea to God was all I could muster. Just then, two figures emerged. Were they fellow missionaries? Americans? My tear-streaked face and trembling body conveyed my predicament without words. They beckoned me to follow, and I clung onto one of them, refusing to let go.

After what felt like an eternity, the distant murmur of voices reached my ears. Prayers for my safety echoed through the jungle, a testament to the concern of my group. I later discovered that the students I had attempted to jog with were scholarship track athletes - a lesson in the importance of definitions, indeed. We did make it home, but only after night had fallen. The darkness of the jungle had given me an unforgettable tale of suspense and survival.

On the eve of the college students' departure, we gathered on the deck to revel in the stunning sunset and reflect on our shared adventures. My close shave with death in the jungle, now a source of much merriment, echoed through our laughter. The quip, "You survived the inner-city of Chicago only to die in the jungle," added to the joviality.

Our gaze shifted skyward as dusk unveiled a spectacle of fruit bats emerging from their caves, taking flight towards the various islands in search of sustenance. Contrary to what you might assume, the fear of bats tangling in one's hair was the least of our concerns. The sight of these winged creatures, more reminiscent of winged Doberman Pinschers than bats, evoked trepidation of being whisked away by their formidable eight-foot wingspans, rather than mere hair entanglement. Reassurances of their harmless fruit-eating habits did little to assuage our fears.

During my final days, I found an unlikely friend in Feardous, a man in his early thirties who had spent his entire life on a neighboring island. With the trust of the missionaries, Feardous became my guide back into the jungle, just like a white person, I went back. He taught me spear fishing and the art of sensing danger, which this time I paid close attention and would have taken notes if I could. One encounter with a protective wild boar mother is etched into my memory, as he thrust me up a tree for safety and fearlessly used his spear and machete to steer the beast away. We conversed in the language of gestures and shared silences, building a bond that transcended the spoken word.

On my last night, I gifted Feardous my clothes and other American possessions, in exchange for which I received a heartfelt hug and a simple "Thank You." The following morning, as I prepared to bid farewell, Feardous introduced me to his father, a prominent chief who wanted to express his gratitude for the impact I had made on his son's life. In an unexpected turn of events, he gifted me my own island, assuring me of a warm welcome if I ever chose to return and visit "my" island. A profound sense of awe enveloped me as I pondered the extraordinary gift and the incredible journey that had brought me here.

Despite these assurances and the honor bestowed upon me, I have not yet returned, and I suspect my island has since been passed on to someone who could make better use of it.

I must preface this tale with an intriguing observation. As we distanced ourselves from the mainland, the Singapore skyscrapers were still faintly visible. It was a startling contrast: the ultra-modern nation of Singapore, perhaps more advanced than the United States, within a stone's throw of some of the most primitive living conditions on the planet. It reminded me of the communities on the "other side of the tracks" back in the states.

The last leg of my journey brought me back to Jakarta, the bustling Indonesian capital, for a couple of days before jetting off to Singapore. I was graciously invited to stay with David, a young man from our English Summer Camp, whose father owned a prominent clothing line comparable to Van Heusen. They were keen on treating me to a shopping spree at their flagship store, a gesture of gratitude for the impact I'd had on David. The trip offered a glimpse of Jakarta's cosmopolitan side, a stark contrast to the rustic setting I'd grown accustomed to during the summer.

But this routine excursion soon transformed into a battle for survival. As we departed the mall, a drizzle evolved into a deluge. The roads, highways, and interstates were inundated. Cars were engulfed by the torrent, swept away like flotsam in a tempestuous sea. The ordinarily 30-minute journey home spiraled into an eight-hour odyssey. Amidst the chaos, David's father confessed he'd never seen such a storm in his 55 years. Despite the circumstances, we pressed on through the night, our spirits undampened by the surrounding turmoil.

Sleep eluded me that night, with only a few precious hours to rest before my flight. David's father had to attend a meeting, so his driver was tasked with taking me to the airport, David accompanying us. Our journey took us onto a high-speed highway, our speedometer nudging past 100 mph, a hair-raising prospect for me, reminding me of my experience of those times on the Autobahn in Germany, no speed limit! Seated in the front, with David in the back, I saw a disaster unfold in slow motion. The car in front of us came to a sudden stop as we hurtled into the vehicle ahead, crashing into its rear. My knees were jammed into the dashboard, leaving a visible indent, while the front of our car crumbled under the impact. Had it not been for our seatbelts, the outcome would have been fatal.

We learned from the ensuing exchanges that a mentally ill woman had wandered onto the highway, sparking the domino effect. Our vehicle, now a mangled mess, was sandwiched between the car we had hit and another that rammed into us from behind. My concerns now shifted from the harrowing accident to the approaching police. I had been cautioned about declaring one's religious beliefs in this predominantly Muslim nation. With my Christian faith potentially acting against me in the eyes of Muslim law enforcement, my predicament was dire. So there we sat, victims of circumstance, waiting for the uncertain repercussions to unfold.

Without warning, I was pulled out of the car and thrust into the back seat of a police vehicle. "Don't worry, Brother Dana," my companions assured me, "they said they will take care of you!" We quickly gave our hugs of goodbye and away I went. In that moment, a flood of questions and doubts consumed my mind. Could I truly trust these individuals? Or were they simply luring me to a secret location, never to be seen again? Fear gripped my heart as I confronted yet another "Welcome to racism" moment, this time within my own Muslim family. Recognizing the judgmental attitudes I had held due to my privileged white Christian beliefs, I fought off the hate I was taught.

To my amazement, these remarkable Muslim men not only ensured my safe journey to the airport but personally escorted me through every line and security checkpoint, guiding me to my seat on the plane. Overwhelmed with gratitude, tears streamed down my face as I reflected on the irony of how I had entered this Muslim country with apprehension and fear, expecting mistreatment as an American Christian. Those tears were not only tears of repentance but also tears for the realization that my Muslim brothers, who had treated me with utmost kindness and respect, would face the very discrimination and hardships in a Christian-dominated America that I had wrongly associated with their faith.

Within a mere two hours, I arrived in Singapore, a nation far more advanced than my own. Every corner of the country was infused with free WiFi, from buses to subway stations and beyond. Sitting in McDonald's, I watched educational shows, and even public transportation offered enlightening content on their TVs. The subway stations, a marvel in themselves, doubled as shelters in times of war with tunnels leading to hospitals. Singapore's beauty captivated me, but it was also a place where strict rules were enforced. Chewing gum was prohibited, and littering could result in severe punishment.

During the following two weeks, I immersed myself in the lives of many young people burdened by depression, suicide, and self-harm—a consequence of the intense pressures they faced within Singapore's highly advanced educational system. The weight of their futures rested on two critical tests in 5th and 8th grade, which determined their career paths. The devastating blow they experienced when test scores dictated their worth and potential left them feeling as if their dreams were shattered. Escaping into the world of drugs became an unfortunate refuge for some.

Amidst the struggles, Singapore's acceptance of diversity shone brightly. Mosques peacefully coexisted alongside Hindu temples, drawing people of all colors and backgrounds to worship in harmony. Rather than competing, they provided spaces for individuals to practice their faith within their respective communities. This mutual respect was a sight to behold. Couples of different skin tones and cultural backgrounds were a common sight, a testament to the inclusivity of Singaporean society.

Though my time in Singapore was brief, the observations and conversations I had left an indelible mark on my heart. It became clear that this nation had much to teach us in America about acceptance, respect, and the celebration of diversity. As I departed Singapore, I carried with me the profound lessons learned, pledging to advocate for unity and understanding in my own homeland.

For the next 26 hours, I embarked on the journey back to America. Exhausted and nursing severe sunburn, I found solace in sleep during each leg of the trip. It wasn't until a week later, when I finally had a moment to sit down and reflect, that I began to sift through the multitude of experiences I had been blessed to encounter. As I looked back, I saw the valuable lessons learned, the reassurances received, and above all, God's unwavering faithfulness throughout it all.

MY LITTLE GUIDING LIGHT

In a world where my social life was as sparse as desert rain, I found solace in the unlikeliest of places. My Fridays would be spent in the mellow hum of Suds Laundromat, while Saturdays were devoted to the mundane, yet essential tasks - cleaning, grocery shopping, and preparing for the week's studies. It might sound bleak, but in truth, this was my life and I cherished it. God had rescued me from an existence that seemed to find no worth in me, so why would I ever crave to return?

One precious treasure that God bestowed upon me was an extraordinary woman named Gina. I first encountered her at Unity Voices of Praise Gospel Choir, a place where souls came together to sing their praises at Moody Bible Institute. Little did I know then that this woman would become my guiding light, a beacon in the night, not only through our three-decade journey in Chicago but even till this very day.

Let me paint you a picture of Gina. She was a petite figure, standing at five foot three, barely touching 100lbs, even when swathed in her winter garments soaking wet. But don't let her physical size fool you - she bore within her a mighty spirit that blended the rich heritage of her Mexican and Korean roots, and a love for God that was infectious to anyone within her vicinity.

In the harmonious ebb and flow of the choir, Gina stood out like a solitary dancer. While the rest of us were moving to the left, she was the bold spirit striding to the right. Her steps were a choreography of her own creation, each twirl and sway a testament to her individuality in interpreting the songs.

Yet, it was her radiant smile, lit by the glow of innocence, that truly captured our hearts. Seeing that smile was like catching a ray of sunshine on a cloudy day, inspiring and heartwarming. It was a quiet encouragement, nudging each of us to dance to the rhythm of our own hearts, to create our own choreography in life's grand performance.

Gina had a profound connection with God, a bond that blessed her with visions and dreams that were nothing short of miraculous. Our relationship was not of parties or fancy soirees; instead, it was forged in the sacred spaces of our walks around Chicago, exploring a new restaurant, canoeing down the Chicago River, or attending a church service. Over the years, we traced the city's veins on foot, meandering along the Magnificent Mile, the beach, down State Street, Grant Park, and even to Lincoln Park Zoo.

One memorable summer, we embarked on a marathon of walks, covering a staggering 25 miles over the 4th of July weekend. During these explorations, we would indulge in innocent window shopping, or pause at newfound eateries, and sometimes, follow divine inspirations to bring words of encouragement to strangers.

During these captivating walks, the timing was never a hindrance to our adventures. Whether it was the late hour of 10pm or the bustling daylight, we would venture on, exploring the city streets. Our pace allowed for leisurely window shopping, discovering new restaurants, and heeding the divine promptings that tugged at our hearts.

There were moments when Gina's intuition was so strong that it demanded immediate attention. She would abruptly halt in her tracks and declare, "I must go into that Starbucks. I have a word for someone." Without hesitation, we would divert our path, following the beckoning of the Holy Spirit. And with unwavering faith, Gina would locate the person whom God had placed on her heart to bless.

It was an awe-inspiring sight to witness. Time and time again, as if guided by the celestial force, Gina would locate the person in need and deliver a message of divine encouragement. The encounters were profound, often accompanied by tears of joy and release. In those precious moments, the transformative power of God's love was palpable, touching the lives of both Gina and the individuals she encountered.

Yet, our journey didn't end there. With renewed spirits, we would continue our walk, savoring the beauty of the cityscape, immersed in the vibrant tapestry of life. Each step taken in faith, every encounter etched in our memories, we discovered the extraordinary in the ordinary, the miraculous in the mundane.

These walks were more than simple strolls; they were journeys of divine connection and purpose. They taught us the boundless possibilities that arise when we align our hearts with God's leading. And as we ventured forth, our souls overflowed with wonder and gratitude for the supernatural moments we were privileged to experience.

So, as you read this account, may it ignite a flame of anticipation within you. May it remind you that even in the midst of a seemingly ordinary walk, there are extraordinary encounters waiting to unfold. Open your heart to the prompting of the divine, for you never know the lives you may touch and the miracles you may witness. Step into the extraordinary, and let your faith guide your path, and Gina truly showed me the way!

Throughout all our cherished moments together, our conversations revolved around God. He was the central focus of our discussions, and we embraced the biblical admonition to sharpen one another, just as iron sharpens iron. In those sacred exchanges, Gina's words held a profound impact on my life, often serving as a guiding light during moments of darkness, confusion, or fear. Her wisdom and encouragement were a balm to my soul.

In Gina's unwavering love for God, I found solace and reassurance. She exemplified a genuine devotion to the Almighty, and her love extended to those around her, including me. It was evident in every interaction, in every word she spoke, and in the compassion that radiated from her heart.

Her words became a source of strength, uplifting my spirit and offering clarity in times of despair. With profound understanding and unwavering faith, she imparted wisdom that illuminated my path and gave me courage to overcome life's challenges. Through her friendship, I discovered the transformative power of God's love, and I was forever grateful for her presence in my life.

In times of joy and in moments of sorrow, Gina remained steadfast, pointing me towards the goodness and grace of God. Her unwavering commitment to the Lord inspired me to deepen my own relationship with Him and to seek His guidance in every aspect of my life.

So, as I reflect upon our shared experiences, I am reminded of the immense impact that Gina had on my spiritual journey. Her love for God and her love for me were intertwined, creating a bond that transcended the boundaries of this earthly realm. I am forever grateful for the privilege of knowing her, for the profound ways in which she sharpened me, and for the enduring legacy of love and faith she left behind.

As you read these words, may they serve as a reminder of the profound impact that a friend, guided by God's love, can have on our lives. May they inspire you to seek out those who sharpen you, and to be a source of strength and encouragement to others in return. And may your journey be enriched by the power of unwavering faith and the transformative love of God.

I will never forget the Thanksgiving of 2016 when Gina agreed to join me on the journey back to my hometown in Minnesota. Over the years, she had formed a close bond with both of my parents. And let me tell you, Gina is an extraordinary traveler, an explorer at heart! She has fearlessly ventured across the globe, navigating the unknown with grace and curiosity. So, a mere 500-mile trip to St. James was a breeze for her.

On that fateful morning, as I picked her up, Gina proposed that we kick off our journey with a hearty breakfast and a prayer. Over our meal, she shared a dream she had the night before. "Maybe it sounds crazy," she said, "but I dreamt that your car wouldn't make it to Minnesota, and neither would I. But dreams can be wild, right? So, let's pray and trust in God's guidance." And so, we did.

As we approached La Crosse, Wisconsin, we felt a surge of relief, knowing that we were three-quarters of the way through our journey, and the car seemed to be running smoothly. However, just as we reached La Crosse, the oil light suddenly illuminated. I knew an oil change was due, but my father, a former mechanic, always ensured that my car was in pristine condition, including fresh oil before I would return to Chicago. Nevertheless, we decided to stop and have the oil changed.

For a while, everything seemed fine. But within the first ten miles after the oil change, the engine light appeared, and within minutes, the car's engine blew! Thankfully, I managed to steer the car to the side of the road, where we sat for the next five-plus hours, waiting for a tow truck. It was moments like these that reminded me why I had sought to leave Minnesota—the long, unforgiving winter season. There we were, on the eve of Thanksgiving, enduring single-digit temperatures.

Eventually, we reached a hotel where we spent the night, anxiously awaiting my father's arrival with a trailer to transport my broken-down car back to Minnesota. Both of us were famished, and luckily, there was one restaurant open 24 hours that still offered delivery. As we savored our meal, Gina mentioned she first started packing her belongings in plastic bags, as she didn't feel like retrieving her suitcases from storage, but heard a voice tell me to get my suitcases. Little did we know the significance of that choice.

As Gina contemplated whether she should still accompany me home, she suddenly developed a severe stomachache. It was a vivid reminder of the dream she had shared earlier, and she ultimately decided to return home while I continued alone to Minnesota. Miraculously, her stomachache subsided.

The next morning, we dropped Gina off at the Greyhound Station, where she boarded the only bus heading to Chicago. My father and I resumed our journey, traveling the remaining two-plus hours to home. Over the next week, I had the opportunity to explore southern Minnesota with my father, searching for a reliable used car. During this time, Gina's dream found unexpected fulfillment as my father and I engaged in deep conversations, experiencing moments of reconciliation and understanding. Our relationship had always been turbulent, filled with love, but often lacking agreement on many matters.

The following year, Gina finally made it to my childhood home for Thanksgiving. It was a moment of immense joy and gratitude as we gathered with my parents, cherishing the blessings of togetherness while hints of laughter and amazement as we reflected on last years trip.

Looking back on this chapter of my life, it serves as a powerful reminder that even in the midst of unexpected challenges and detours, God's guiding hand is always at work. He orchestrates divine connections, unveils hidden blessings, and brings forth transformative experiences. Our journey was about more than just a broken-down car and missed destinations; it was about the deeper lessons of trust, resilience, and the enduring power of love. And that's why I call Gina, "My Little Guiding Light"!

I CROSSED OVER THE LINE

As I pen down the words of this book, I am engulfed by the reminder of God's unwavering benevolence. I am transported back to that pivotal moment in 1990 when I heard Him whisper, "I love you," preventing me from a suicidal precipice. I recall my solemn vow, "Father, my life is yours now, I owe it all to you." Reflecting back, it appears He took my words quite literally and embarked on a mission with them. While my sufferings have never paralleled those of Paul, I find a strange resonance in his narrative.

In the book of Acts, chapter 9, Paul is en route to persecute and eliminate followers of The Way, heedless of his divine calling. On the Road to Damascus, he is confronted and redirected. Similarly, I was walking a path where my white privilege was knowingly and unknowingly wreaking havoc on my Black brothers and sisters through prejudice, injustice, racism – my white supremacist beliefs. Just like Paul, I heard His voice while my companions kept walking, oblivious to the divine intervention.

Echoes of Acts 9:15 resonate within me, when the Lord says to Ananias, "Go! This man is my chosen instrument to proclaim my name to the Gentiles and their kings and to the people of Israel. I will show him how much he must suffer for my name." Just as Paul was dispatched to Ananias, I was blessed to be sent to my Black family. Paul was rendered blind for three days; in contrast, my blindness spanned nearly 30 years, with the profound repercussions of racism still eluding my full comprehension.

It should have dawned on me sooner that the opposition I was facing at church was a foretaste of the resistance I would later encounter from my own white family, blood and non blood. I distinctly recall the wave of optimism that swept over us when President Obama was elected. During a conversation with some elders of a church in southern Minnesota, they inquired about my well-being and the progress of my ministry. As I recounted the newfound hope that had breathed life into my Black family, especially the young men, a veil of silence descended upon our conversation.

A week or so later, a phone call jolted me. "Dana, we fear your ministry seems more dedicated to serving Obama than Jesus! Perhaps you should consider working for him instead," they suggested. Subsequently, they withdrew their monthly support for my mission.

Another church, consumed by curiosity about the source of my "spiritual teaching," asked me about my choice of congregation in Chicago. "A COGIC one," I replied. They were unfamiliar with the Church of God in Christ, and their ignorance about this Black-founded denomination led to questions about its legitimacy and teachings. Their skepticism was rooted in a deeply entrenched belief in white supremacy. They held firm to the notion that White American Evangelicals were God's chosen ones to disseminate the Gospel of Jesus Christ worldwide. An air of intellectual superiority pervaded their words, "We are the enlightened ones, Dana!" One church leader even wanted to interrogate my Pastor about our theological beliefs!

A particularly poignant instance involves my friend Doug who he and his wife Heather were instrumental in saving my life early on in my journey, as mentioned previously in this book. Together, Doug and I rented a minivan and took six young men from my youth group on a field trip to Minnesota. It was a joyous and thrilling experience, but it also unveiled an unsettling amount of racism.

One comment, in particular, stands out: "Oh Dana, these boys are not like the rest of them." To which I responded, "The rest of who?" The vague reply that followed was, "Oh Dana, you know what we're talking about." But in truth, I did not. It was their first encounter with a group of young Black men, so exactly who were they comparing them to? Their attempt to separate these young men from a stereotyped group based on their color was a glaring exposure of deep-seated racial bias, showing that the tentacles of racism can reach even into the most casual and seemingly benign interactions.

I spent my childhood days in a house situated opposite Memorial Park, a delightful recreational area embellished with a bandstand, two playgrounds, two picnic houses, and sprawling green spaces. It also boasted a baseball field, complete with a spacious parking lot. My formative years were filled with exhilarating memories of this park, notably the thrill of learning to drive a garden tractor under my father's guidance. He would permit us kids to steer it around the parking lot when the park was void of activities. Sometimes, we would hitch a small wagon to it and ferry younger children around, much to their delight.

Sunday afternoon after we returned from church and ate dinner, my father asked the guys from Chicago if they would want a go at driving his garden tractor. This was an enlightening moment for my parents as they confronted racism in an explicit manner. Antwane, one of the guys, had barely started driving before several police cars swarmed our peaceful park. The reason, we were told, was a complaint about 'kids driving a tractor in the park.' "They are driving in the parking lot, just like my children have for years," my dad argued, recognizing the discriminatory undertone, "Oh, I see, the issue is that Antwane is black."

Even before I broach the topic of family, I must share one of the most heart-wrenching betrayals I experienced from the very people who took me to SonShine Festival, where I fostered a spiritual bond with God. Evangelicals would phrase it as the event where I invited Christ into my heart and got saved. The joy in the car as we returned home was palpable - they had hoped my commitment to Christ would be the crowning achievement of their invitation. They had celebrated my decision to live for Christ, supported my journey to Moody, but the moment I was called to serve God in the Black inner-city, their support crumbled. A lifelong friendship ended abruptly. The celebrations ceased. They even advised my mother to "get Dana away from the blacks" during casual store encounters.

This rejection brought back a warning from Betty back in 1995, stating that crossing a certain line would be irreversible. That line, it appears, was becoming too entangled with the Black community. Subsequently, I was ostracized, one church at a time, no longer included in their prayers or offered their support. My own aunt, who had endorsed a video of Bill Cosby lecturing young Black men on decorum, severed ties with me after I suggested that we should first address our own familial issues before criticizing others.

The severity of this metaphorical line I had crossed was hammered home following my father's passing in November 2021. During his Celebration of Life service, which I conducted, several extended family members abruptly left. Others walked out immediately after the service concluded. The hateful messages I received labeled me a disgrace and urged me to "go back to your black family," a suggestion I was more than happy to comply with. Today, I maintain contact with a single cousin and my mother. God, throughout this ordeal, has been a comforting presence, reminding me that "your family are those who do my will." This taught me that blood relations and family can be two vastly different things.

Despite Betty's warning, I had hoped for my family to be different, but it seems racism and white privilege have infiltrated our DNA. The pain I feel is less about personal rejection and more about the contempt shown towards my chosen family - my Black family - whom I hold dear. Following the funeral, I made a vow never to return home, not even to bury my mother, who now comprehends the depth of this hatred. Betty was right, once I crossed that line, there is no returning.

BRING BACK WILLIE LYNCH

Throughout my life, the pain that has cut me the deepest wasn't from the harsh words hurled at me, the shattered bottles assaulting my head, the heart-breaking loss of my beloved dogs, the chilling invasions of my personal space through burglary or even the loss of my blood family. Rather, the deepest agony has been borne from witnessing my white family cling to their privilege, stubbornly upholding and bringing back the principles reminiscent of Willie Lynch.

Who was Willie Lynch, you ask? He is a controversial figure from history, believed to have delivered a speech in 1712 on controlling and manipulating enslaved African people in the American colonies. This speech is immortalized in what's known as the "Willie Lynch Letter," allegedly outlining methods to maintain control over enslaved people by exacerbating divisions based on age, skin tone, and social status as well as other tools he brought in his bag of evil.

Whether real or fabricated, the letter has been central to contemporary discussions about the enduring legacies of slavery. It underscores how divisions were intentionally sown among enslaved people to maintain control over them. Again, in spite of your opinion on this document, I want to share the truth of how I have seen it working and even the reinstating of it by my white family.

Nevertheless, in our current era, I observe these divisive principles resurfacing. Lynch's purported letter claims, "I HAVE A FULL PROOF METHOD FOR CONTROLLING YOUR BLACK SLAVES. I guarantee every one of you that, if installed correctly, IT WILL CONTROL THE SLAVES FOR AT LEAST 300 HUNDREDS YEARS." We're now well past that 300-year mark, and our Black community has been valiantly combating racism since this nation began.

The alleged method of Lynch was predicated on the idea of amplifying disparities among enslaved people to incite conflict. As I observe the present, it's distressing to note how this approach still fuels divisions today. Discord emerges along lines of skin tone, geographical divide, and even the construct of "good hair." Among my Black sisters, this phrase is used to describe hair texture akin to that of a Caucasian woman, instigating unnecessary comparison and friction.

We've also witnessed how these divisions have estranged the older generation from the younger, creating an environment ripe for intervention by external authorities. These authorities, likened to the police or the slave masters of old, are called upon to manage these communities. Yet their presence often leads to further injustice. This injustice has placed our fathers and men in our prison systems or grave, leaving our younger men without role models and the protection only a father can give. Meanwhile, my white kin seem intent on saving their own after egregious acts.

I've unearthed the hidden history of places like Cabrini Green, a history that the sitcom Good Times didn't reveal. Back then, when employment was scarce for Black men, their families were invited to move into housing projects like Cabrini Green with one catch—the men couldn't live with their families. This stipulation was a devious strategy to splinter the Black family unit, reminiscent of the horrific practices during slavery when children were sold off to other plantations, and fathers were used as breeders across various estates.

Drugs in inner-city America, lynchings, the horrific use of infant slaves as alligator bait, and the exploitation of enslaved people to build this nation — all these atrocities pale in comparison to the distrust and envy sown between them with the intention THAT YOUR SLAVES TRUST AND DEPEND ON US. THEY MUST LOVE, RESPECT AND TRUST ONLY US. The enduring effects of this destructive manipulation bring me to tears as I have seen and witness this horrible reality.

Willie Lynch is said to have outlined six principles for long-term success and economic strategy. The first is perhaps the most striking. "Both horse and black man are no good to the economy in the wild or natural state." You were brought here for our economic benefit—whether that meant toiling in cotton fields, serving in houses, or entertaining us with your talents. Slavery was more than a provisional plan; it formed the backbone of our economy.

Every system — justice, correctional, educational, spiritual — was designed to mold you in our image, making it impossible for you to return to your life before captivity. You were painted with an indoctrinated fear: the wild black man, seeking freedom, "might kill you in your sleep. You cannot rest. They sleep while you are awake, and are awake while you are asleep. They are DANGEROUS near the family house."

This statement hit close to home for me when a white female juror in Mike's case was asked, "What made you believe Mike was guilty?" Her response was, "Anyone who is out at 1:00 in the morning and not working is up to no good!" She concluded that Mike's late-night presence implied he was involved in the heinous crimes of raping and murdering two white women. This prejudiced mindset underscores how deeply ingrained stereotypes or thoughts of the black man being a wild dangerous animal has influenced our perception of guilt and innocence of the black man.

This fear birthed the phenomena of 'white flight,' redlining, cross-burning in yards, segregated schools, wrongful convictions, and lynchings. It justified the immediate shooting of unarmed black men, the destruction of black communities with introduced drugs, and even the bombing of entire black cities like "Black Wall Street". The restrictions on voting and bearing arms were all crafted and enforced to ensure the 'wild black man' would never claim his freedom. "Above all, you cannot get them to work in this natural state. Hence both the horse and the black man must be broken; that is breaking them from one form of mental life to another." The narrative painted the enslaved black man as the dangerous one, not the white man who kidnapped, shipped, enslaved, raped, beat, and killed.

We have proudly celebrated our white heritage, labeling ourselves as the "great pioneers" who ventured forth to explore, establish homes, and build communities and towns. In stark contrast, we have dismissed our Black and Native American family as "savages." However, it is undeniable that it was the so-called "great pioneers" who decimated the homes, communities, and towns of those we encountered on our path. Were they truly "great pioneers" or rather "great evil mad-men"? The answer becomes abundantly clear when we confront the truth that our education system has conveniently omitted. It is a sobering realization that forces us to reevaluate our perceptions and acknowledge the deep-rooted indoctrination that has obscured the truth.

One contemporary example of this lies in the public humiliation of Colin Kaepernick. According to Lynch, "When it comes to breaking the uncivilized black slave, use the same process, but vary the degree and step up the pressure, so as to do a complete reversal of the mind." Kaepernick was seen as a threat, a restless spirit discontent with the killing of young black men at the hands of white racist cops. To white America, his choice to take a knee during the National Anthem was uncivilized, a display of disrespect towards the American flag. Kaepernick needed to be made an example of lest his actions inspired others to challenge injustice. Consequently, white America did everything it could to strip him of dignity, tar and feather him, and ultimately tear him apart. And yet, he rose! His endurance stands as a testament to the resilience of the black man and the continuing fight for justice and equality.

"Take the black female and run a series of tests on her to see if she will submit to your desires willingly. Test her in every way, because she is the most important factor for good economics." This alarming statement is directly from Lynch's purported words, further stating that a woman should be beaten with a bull whip to ensure she would teach her offspring submission to labor.

I've witnessed the reality of many single-parent households among my young men I have mentored though out my years, which stands in stark contrast to the stable two-parent homes my white classmates grew up in. I've seen firsthand the struggle of single black mothers striving to raise their sons into men. This observation isn't a critique of the immense strength and capability of black mothers - far from it. In fact, I know a mother of seven children, five of them boys, all of whom are successful today. She, like many other single black mothers, has performed admirably in the dual roles of mom and dad.

However, this system has labored to make black women dependent on white society for necessities like food, shelter, and even protection. As a result, she often raises her children, especially her sons, to rely on white society. The cycle of mental indoctrination carries on. As Lynch's alleged words put it, "In this frozen psychological state of independence, she will raise her MALE and female offspring in reversed roles. For FEAR of the young male's life, she will psychologically train him to be MENTALLY WEAK and DEPENDENT, but PHYSICALLY STRONG. Because she has become psychologically independent, she will train her FEMALE offsprings to be psychologically independent. What have you got? You've got the black WOMAN OUT FRONT AND THE BLACK MAN BEHIND AND SCARED. This is a perfect situation of sound sleep and economic." This might help you understand why Colin Kaepernick's protest was so quickly shut down. His strength and independence threatened a system that thrives on mental subordination.

Let's shed light on a profound truth found within the Willie Lynch Letters. Regardless of whether they originated from an actual speech or just as written correspondence, their effects are undeniably present today, and you'll start noticing them too. Consider this passage, "WE MUST COMPLETELY ANNIHILATE THE MOTHER TONGUE of both the new black and the new mule and institute a new language that involves the new life's work of both. You know language is a peculiar institution. It leads to the heart of a people."

This revelation should be heart-wrenching! We've effectively erased the language, history, and true identity of the African American community. Today, white America fiercely defends their narrative, battling against the introduction of "Critical Race Theory" into our education system. They have resisted by legally banning it, seeking to prevent it from influencing our indoctrination education system originally designed to mold African Americans into a prescribed image, all while conveniently omitting significant aspects of our shared history.

Critical Race Theory not only uncovers the genuine history of African Americans, but it also brings to light the darker parts of our own past. Our true history is reflected in the distorted image we've projected onto the African American community. It was our own malice that crafted such a flawed portrayal. It was our wickedness that we transferred onto our black family. Critical Race Theory promises to unveil these truths, and also to reintroduce the true identity of African Americans before their capture, a topic I will explore further in the final chapter.

The letter further emphasizes, "If you take a slave, if you teach him all about your language, he will know all your secrets, and then he is no longer a slave, for you can't fool him any longer. Being a fool is one of the basic ingredients to maintaining the slavery system." This may make you wonder why there was such a struggle to keep our schools segregated in our history. Unfortunately, today, if total physical desegregation can't be quickly achieved, efforts to exclude Critical Race Theory will help foster intellectual segregation until our schools can fully integrate segregation again, and don't think this is not a goal of white supremacy.

This principle takes the concept of language to a deeper level, suggesting a specific language should be used to reinforce the societal roles of master and slave. "Values are created and transported by communication through the body of the language. A total society has many interconnected value systems. All the values in the society have bridges of language to connect them for orderly working in the society."

This language creates a particular discourse that constantly reinforces America's societal hierarchy and value system, where the African American community is reduced to their "slave" status, thus remaining at the bottom. This is the impetus behind the creation of the "Slave Bible," which emphasized verses commanding slaves to honor, respect, and even express gratitude to their white masters, who purportedly saved them from their ungodly traditions.

It's why African American men are stereotyped as "thugs," why African American women are labeled as "angry," and why the term "boy" has been used derogatorily towards African American men of all ages. It explains the harmful power behind the use of racial slurs. Each of these components work in tandem to uphold the structures of white supremacy and our value system.

Like I've said before, even if this letter is deemed fiction, it doesn't negate the fact that this nation has employed these principles to uphold white supremacy. So, what exactly is white supremacy? It is the belief that white people are inherently superior to individuals of other races and therefore should exert dominance in all aspects of society: social, political, educational, historical, and industrial. This belief upholds and defends any power and privilege held by white individuals. White supremacy is not a truth; it is a fabricated concept that we have turned into a harsh reality for our black family members.

This reality is intertwined with white privilege. It grants us white people a set of advantages and immunities that work to their benefit while simultaneously disadvantaging our black family. White privilege can persist even without the conscious awareness of white individuals, and it serves to maintain the racial hierarchy in our country. No white person in this country is exempt from this privilege, even our poor unvalued white family members still have privilege over the black man.

President Trump's assertions about the bias, one-sidedness, injustice, political motivation, and corruption within various systems of authority in this nation are correct. This corruption has always existed, but never before has this system been used against one of its own. White men have been absolved of their bloody hands in perpetrating incredible injustices, while our innocent black family continues to suffer under the weight of these actions. And then sadly white fragility keeps rears its head every time anything associated with or around white supremacy is brought up to a white family member.

So now you may ask, what is white fragility? Well, it is when even a minimum amount of racial stress becomes intolerable, triggering a range of defensive moves to include the outward display of emotions such as anger, fear, and guilt, and behaviors such as argumentation, and disrespectfully walking away from the situation. I put it this way. My white family are more concerned with their little toe being stepped on by talks about racism as it kills our black family!

Now, you may ask, what is white fragility? Let me be bold and clear. White fragility is when even the tiniest hint of racial stress becomes unbearable, leading to defensive reactions that involve displaying emotions like anger, fear, and guilt, and engaging in behaviors such as argumentation and disrespectfully walking away from the situation or conversation. Allow me to emphasize this: My white family is more focused on the discomfort of their little toe being stepped on during discussions about racism, while our black family are suffering and dying from racism!

In closing out this chapter there is just no way even this book can hold all the thoughts and emotions I want to share with you about the depth of racism and white supremacy in our nation. It's so ingrained in our society that it's the blood running through our veins. I hope that what we've explored so far has opened your eyes and touched your heart. This is a big topic, one that is very heavy and complicated. But remember, it's important to confront these hard truths, to ask tough questions, and to learn from them. My plea is to my white family to work to understand more, to do better, and to inspire change so our beloved black family are loved and valued as they so much deserve.

NOT CURSED, BUT CHOSEN

I needed to take a deep breath before I was able to start this final chapter. The whirlwind of thoughts swirling in my mind made it difficult to find the right starting point, to give due justice to the journey that brought me here and hoping to share everything my Father would have me say. Over the years, I had borne witness to the gnawing prejudice ingrained in all of our systems especially the justice system—a system designed seemingly for 'just us' white people. It was evident how our correctional institutions, the prisons and jails scattered across the country, mirrored today's cotton fields, managed either by the government or private owners.

The specter of racism was also prominent in our educational system. I saw how it systematically set our Black students up for failure, from the unequal testing and examination procedures to the disparity in access to modern curriculum and technology—a fact unmasked by the pandemic not too long ago. It was disheartening to learn that the decision to construct more prisons was based on the test scores of Black students in 6th to 8th grades, thereby ensuring a continuous pipeline to prison and enough beds to house them.

I've seen the injustice permeating our social system, from the postcards of smiling white families standing in front of a Black man being lynched and burned simultaneously, all on a quiet Sunday afternoon after church service. The disturbing images and footage of the brutalities endured by my

Black family during the Civil Rights Movement, the savage attacks by police dogs, the merciless blasts from water hoses, the beatings with clubs, are etched into my memory.

I observed how the slogan 'Make America Great Again' was twisted into a vehicle to re-establish the shackles of Black servitude. From the derogatory language emanating from the White House—branding them as 'thugs' and 'people from shithole countries'—to the terrifying sight of white supremacists attacking the Capitol, I witnessed a terrifying distortion of reality where a Black man taking a knee seemed a greater offense.

The horrifying pride of white men chasing down a Black jogger to kill him was not lost on me. Nor was the haunting frequency of white police officers suffocating innocent Black men to death—either by pinning them to the ground or placing a knee of hatred on their necks, methodically extinguishing their lives with no thought of their actions except the feeling of achieving the goal of exterminating yet another black man.

For years, it was a bitter pill to swallow, acknowledging the deep-seated hatred against my Black family. Hate is a strong word, but when you examine the way this nation has treated them—from the moment they were torn away from their homeland over 400 years ago to the present day— there's no better term to describe it. If we label leaders like Putin, Hitler, and Saddam Hussein as embodiments of hate for their deeds, how can we ignore our own 400 plus years atrocities? Who could perpetrate such malevolence, only to stifle their victims' voices to uphold white supremacy?

It was this profound question that expanded my search beyond the confines of American racism, into understanding the root cause of this global hatred. I sought answers from God Himself, delving into His word to find a solution. For if we could identify the root cause, we could eradicate this malignant weed permanently.

During my time in Bible college, I came across the infamous reference to the 'Curse of Ham' in the Book of Genesis. This curse was supposedly placed on Ham's son Canaan by Noah, in the aftermath of a shameful act perpetrated by Ham. Over centuries, this text has been used by white Christians to justify the brutal enslavement and treatment of Black people, attributing their dark skin to this curse, hence marking them fit for enslavement.

I sought answers, delving into the white-walled offices of white Christian professors and pastors, hoping to uncover the truth. However, instead of clarity, I was met with a recurring narrative. When I confronted them with the stark reality, asking, "Why is it that our black family devotes more time to church and worshiping God in one service than we white Christians do in a month, yet they continue to face hatred and mistreatment?" And, if the blood of Jesus was shed to break all curses, why not the Curse of Ham?" I received nothing but empty platitudes that left my thirst for truth unquenched. Even as confusion clouded my mind and more questions arose, their ultimate response remained consistent: "Yes, slavery was regrettable, but at least our Black family was saved from the sins of worshiping false gods and engaging in witchcraft. And although they may have to live under this mistreatment we must remember Romans when it says; "The sufferings we have now are nothing compared to the great glory that will be shown to us." Now I walked out mad, "easy for you to say when you're not the one suffering"!

In those moments, I couldn't help but wonder: Is this truly the best explanation they can offer? Is this the extent of their understanding and empathy? How can we claim to follow a God of love and justice, yet perpetuate such harmful narratives that justify the mistreatment of an entire race? The more I pondered, the more I realized that these answers were not satisfactory, nor were they rooted in the truth I sought.

It became evident that the narrative of the Curse of Ham served as a convenient excuse, a twisted justification for the systemic oppression and discrimination faced by our black family. It was a false truth that allowed the perpetrators, us whites, to absolve themselves of guilt and maintain their position of power and privilege. As I stood there, surrounded by the echoes of empty explanations, I couldn't help but question the foundations of my faith and the integrity of those who propagated such beliefs. But my search for truth continued, and I refuse to settle for complacency or half-truths. I am determined to challenge the narratives and theology I was taught in Christianity.

Over these years my frustration only intensified, for I knew there was an answer out there. God wouldn't instill this drive within me for nothing. This search for answers escalated as I witnessed countless innocent young Black men being lynched by police, with my white family, especially my white Evangelical Family dismissively crying out, "If you would only just comply!" I still would like to know where all my white pro-lifers were to join us in the protesting of these abortions taking the lives of innocent black family members?

July 17, 2014, remains forever seared into my soul. The world was presented with another horrific example of America's racism when Eric Garner pleaded "I can't breathe" 11 times as NYPD Officer Daniel Pantaleo pinned him to the ground on suspicion of illegally selling cigarettes. Garner's death was ruled a homicide, but a grand jury decided not to prosecute Pantaleo, who was later dismissed by the NYPD.

Despite Garner's plea for life's most basic need, he was denied even that. My anger and frustration were metamorphosing into bitterness. I decided to express my thoughts via a video on Facebook titled "My thoughts on the killings of our young black men." In this seven-minute video, I compared America's treatment of Black men to how ancient Egypt sought to suppress the Hebrew population by murdering their male offspring.

Pharaoh's orders to the midwives— "When you help the Hebrew women in childbirth, look at the child when you deliver it. If it's a boy, kill it, but if it's a girl, let it live."— was a chilling mirror to America's ongoing assault on Black men for nearly 400 years. I also the Hebrew woman like today's black woman to be strong and healthy, more than the white woman. "The Hebrew women aren't like the Egyptian women; they're vigorous. Before the midwife can get there, they've already had the baby."

I had no idea that this video would resonate with millions after going viral. The response from the Black community was overwhelming, it was liberating to know that my words helped them feel acknowledged by a white individual, recognizing America's gravest sin—white supremacy!

The response from my white family was markedly different. I received a barrage of derogatory comments and threats, labeling me as a traitor and racial slurs. But instead of shaking me, these comments only solidified the truth behind my comparison and the prevailing mindset within my white community.

In the midst of these calls and emails, I saw yet another tragedy on August 9, 2014. Michael Brown, an unarmed Black teenager, was shot to death by Ferguson, Missouri police officer Darren Wilson despite Brown raising his hands during the police chase and pleading, "Don't shoot." The grand jury decided not to indict Wilson, sparking civil unrest and protests in the community.

August 9th was a day that forever left an indelible mark on my life. It stood as a pivotal point in my history, a moment that would reverberate through the next thirty years and beyond. On that day, I returned home carrying a heavy heart, burdened by a bitter disappointment. Once again, the pervasive shadow of racism had reared its ugly head and claimed victory over a young man I had been mentoring for years.

With every step toward my home, frustration throbbed within me, pulsating louder and louder. As I crossed the threshold, I was swallowed by a torrent of despair, my spirit anchored down by the ceaseless recurrence of injustice that seemed to pollute my every day. I had reached my limit, completely overwhelmed by the relentless, unforgiving reality of racism.

I stood at the precipice of my bedroom door, my heart heavy and my mind in turmoil. As I processed my surroundings, a chilling realization unfurled within me. My lips parted, and with a voice laden with anguish, I cried out, "If you, God, are against them than what hope can I bring! You call me here to suffer watching those I love be killed? This is also why your church is steeped in racism. You a racist God yourself!" My words echoed, their bitterness bouncing off the walls.

"So, damn you and damn your religion!" I continued, my voice cracking with the intensity of my emotions. "I refuse to serve a racist God!" With that, I hurled my Bible across the room, watching as it tumbled through the air, an embodiment of my disillusionment and despair. My whole life was to serve God by seeking to understand the pain of racism, and this is what it came too, You?

Time stretched in that dark room, echoing the somber notes of my past confrontation with suicidal thoughts. Had I truly devoted all these years serving a racist God? This gnawing question consumed me, yet in the midst of my internal turmoil, a different voice, potent and undeniable, One I have heard before, rose above my tumultuous thoughts: "No, son, they are not cursed. They are my Precious Chosen Children." He spoke Deuteronomy 28.

In that moment, I sprang from my spot, my heart pounding as I retrieved my discarded Bible from the floor. My fingers hastily turned the pages to find the appointed chapter. The first part, under the header 'Blessings on Obedience', didn't strike a chord. But as I delved into the second half, 'Curses on Disobedience', I felt a jolt of recognition. The Divine One, the Most High Yah, was revealing to me the undeniable truth about my black family: they were and are His Precious Chosen Children, originally known as the true Hebrews of the Bible!

With a racing heart, I sat on my bed, attempting to decipher the last verses through tear-blurred eyes. My emotions were a whirlwind - shock, relief, awe. The Almighty Yah Himself had unveiled the answer that had eluded me for so long. This was the truth that would illuminate the path to liberation for my black family. It was a revelation that brought understanding to my spirit, and a message I was now equipped to proclaim to set my black family free; "You are not cursed, but Chosen"!

FROM MY HEART...

First let me just put it out there, please forgive me of my grammatical errors, misspellings, and punctuation issues that may mar the pages of this book. I hope these imperfections will be overshadowed by the purpose of my writing—to step across the line, to raise my hand against injustice, to abandon the comfort of the white palace, and to never look back as I have placed my hand on the plow! I pray, with holy boldness, as my mentor Aloysius taught me so well, that I would stand before you to speak the unvarnished truth of the unspeakable atrocities inflicted upon you, our beloved black family.

To you, my precious black family, I extend my sincerest apologies. I am sorry for my own complicity and for the role my forefathers played in tarnishing your lives, dismantling your families, eroding your communities, and devaluing your inherent worth. I am aware that every time you and your ancestors pulled yourselves up by your bootstraps, we, European white Americans not only destroyed your progress but also snatched away your very boots you worked for, boots I was given.

In the midst of this acknowledgement, I offer my heartfelt gratitude. Thank you for the profound lessons you have taught me—lessons of loyalty, resilience, determination, strength, perseverance, and above all, the transformative power of forgiveness and love. I am immensely grateful for the gift of your forgiveness, for embracing me as one of your own, and for extending an invitation to the sacred gatherings to include your barbecues. By bestowing upon me my Black Card, you have made me feel like a cherished member of your family.

I want to acknowledge the undeniable truth: your ancestors' free labor greatly benefited me and my white family. While this came at the expense of your well-being, I must admit that I have reaped the rewards. Countless inventions that have shaped modern society, such as the elevator, the guitar, stop lights, cell phones, and the light bulb, were products of your ancestors' ingenuity. Moreover, your innovations, including the x-ray, the pacemaker, and groundbreaking research on cancer and leukemia, have played a vital role in preserving and improving our lives. Without your contributions, America would not be the prosperous nation it is today, at least for the white population.

I also want to express my sincere apologies for the injustice that prevailed in the music industry for so many years. Your ancestors' incredible talents and gifts were often suppressed and excluded from the airwaves. Instead, these songs were appropriated and popularized by white artists like Elvis Presley, who became renowned for their distinctive sound. It is a painful truth that your ancestors' influence and contributions were disregarded, denying them the credit and recognition they deserved.

I am sorry for the injustices perpetrated against you, my black family throughout history. I am committed to acknowledging and rectifying these wrongs, and to fostering a society that celebrates and uplifts all voices, regardless of race. Your resilience, creativity, and immeasurable contributions have enriched our world in countless ways. It is long overdue that we recognize and honor your incredible legacy and make things right, monetarily.

Over these years, in your presence, I have witnessed the beauty of a community that uplifts and supports one another, even in the face of unimaginable adversity. Your unwavering spirit, your celebration of culture and heritage, and your unwavering commitment to justice and equality inspire me to be a better advocate, ally, and friend. I stand beside you with stedfast dedication, ready to amplify your voices, dismantle systemic racism, and foster a future where the sins of the past no longer define our shared humanity and no longer affect your seed.

Together, let us continue this journey of healing, reconciliation, and transformation. May our collective efforts pave the way for a world where every individual, regardless of their race, is valued, respected, and afforded equal opportunities. With gratitude and love, I offer my hand as we walk this path together, knowing that only through unity and understanding can we create lasting change.

As stated in "Lift Every Voice and Sing";

Facing the rising sun of our new day begun,
Let us march on 'til **YOUR** victory is won!

Your Brother, from another Mother,
Dana

WORKS CITED

Angelou, Maya. Still I Rise. Random House, 1978.
Lynch, Willie. The Willie Lynch Letter And The Making Of
     A Slave, Classic House Books, 2008
Shakur, Tupac. The Rose That Grew from Concrete. Pocket
     Books, 1999.